AF531581

MANAGEMENT OF DISTANCE EDUCATION

MANAGEMENT OF DISTANCE EDUCATION

Dinesh Chander Sharma

ANMOL PUBLICATIONS PVT. LTD.
NEW DELHI - 110 002 (INDIA)

ANMOL PUBLICATIONS PVT. LTD.
H.O.: 4374/4B, Ansari Road, Daryaganj
New Delhi - 110 002
Ph.: 23261597, 23278000
B.O.: No. 1015, Ist Main Road, BSK III Stage
III Phase, III Block
Bangalore - 560 085 (India)
Visit us at: www.anmolpublications.com

Management of Distance Education

First Published, 2005

ISBN 81-261-2635-3

ICSSR Consultant: Professor Dr. J.L. Azad

[The publication of this book has been financially supported by the Indian Council of Social Science Research, New Delhi. However, the responsibility for the facts stated and conclusions reached is entirely that of the Author and the ICSSR bears no responsibility for them.]

PRINTED IN INDIA

Published by J.L. Kumar for Anmol Publications Pvt. Ltd., New Delhi - 110 002 and Printed at Mehra Offset Press, Delhi.

CONTENTS

PREFACE

Education has been instrumental in disseminating various accomplishments of human civilization throughout human history in different forms. It has been recognized time and again that education plays a crucial role in producing and transferring knowledge and skills in society. Education contributes to economic growth, poverty reduction, development of mental faculties, and growth of general awareness in all human societies.

The education systems in India have seen many changes i.e. from Gurukul, Madarsa and Convent/Public School education to the era of distance education and e-education. Transformation of education system is a continuous process. As is evident from the past that conventional education system was inadequate in meeting the educational needs of the people which gave birth to correspondence/distance education as an alternative channel of education.

Distance education system has acquired the status of an important social organization after its fruitful existence of more than two decades. It is making a valuable contribution in fulfilling the educational objectives of the society, with its advent as a viable supplement to the conventional education system.

The Govt. of Andhra Pradesh took initiative and established first Open University the "Andhra Pradesh Open University" in the country (now renamed as Dr. B.R. Ambedkar Open University). Encouraged by the success of establishment of an open university at State level, the Union Government also established "Indira Gandhi National Open University" on September 20, 1985.

The quality of educational programmes offered by distance education system depends upon management and structures of distance education system. The management of distance educational system is nothing but the adaptation of a coordinated approach of all the functions/subsystems involved in design and delivery of its learners.

The management of distance education involves four key elements of management i.e. planning, organizing, implementing and controlling. The success of quality initiative in distance education is greatly dependent on the application of management principles and practices to the system. A system is created with noble object but due to various inherent human weaknesses, the system looses its spirit if management systems and procedures/processes are not followed in letter and spirit.

Each system attains its vision, mission, and objectives through convergence and submergence of its subsystems. The distance education also needs supplementation and complementation of other systems like Human Resources, Financial Resources, Marketing of Services, Integration of Technologies, etc. In India, it is visible that education overpowers all other systems and are not seen performing and contributing independently as a system, which leads to inefficiencies and inadequacies in the educational system that holds true for distance education system as well.

The present study intends to make an effort to appraise the Management of Distance Education System in India with specific reference to Indira Gandhi National Open University, an apex body and a national university in the field of distance education by systems approach and to evaluate the effectiveness of each subsystem.

This study is presented in 9 chapters. Chapter I, highlights the need for distance education and its nature, its history and growth, reviews the researches in the area of distance education and describes the research procedure. Chapter II, in brief, highlights the main objectives, features, organizational structure and authorities of the Indira Gandhi National Open University. It also traces the history and growth of the University in terms of student enrolment, number of programmes offered and revenue generation. In chapter III, a conceptual model of management of distance education has been developed. Chapter IV examines the strategic planning processes and practices adopted at Indira Gandhi National Open University. Chapter V makes an attempt to evaluate the administrative, financial and library systems of the university. Chapter VI inquires about the design and development of academic programmes and management of media support system. Chapter VII provides an insight on the status of research function in the University. Chapter VIII apprises on the student registration and database management system, material delivery system, student support services of the University and its student assessment and evaluation system. Finally, Chapter IX presents the overall findings of study and suggest measures for efficient and effective management of distance education system in IGNOU.

The present exploratory research endeavour may not provide a comprehensive analysis of all possible issues but it does offer a penetrating insight into the issues involved in the management of distance education system.

Distance/Open education universities and institutes shall find the findings of the present study useful and beneficial for strengthening the management of their institutes and in delivering quality education to the vast majority of the students.

—Author

Chapter 1

INTRODUCTION

ROLE OF HIGHER EDUCATION

Education has been instrumental in disseminating various accomplishments of human civilization throughout human history in different forms. It has been recognized time and again that education plays a crucial role in producing and transferring knowledge and skills in society. Education contributes to economic growth, poverty reduction, development of mental faculties, and the growth of general awareness in all human societies.

Several scholars have highlighted role of education in society development. It is well established that nations with high literacy rate and good educational infrastructure have made significant progress in standards of living, health care, equal distribution of resources and their by in total improvement in the social pattern; thus life is more comfortable and enjoyable in those countries, which are educationally developed.

Education structure in India is an old three-tier system i.e. primary, secondary and higher education. It originated from the Calcutta University Commission of 1917-1919, which recommended introduction of matriculation, intermediate and first-degree examinations. The Commission recommended that first-degree course should be of three-year duration. The Radhakrishnan University Commission of 1948-49 repeated the idea with the hope that three year degree course will raise the standards of higher education.[1]

Altbatch P.G. (1987)[2] states that "Higher education constitutes a very important institution in the third World context not only because it trains elites and provides the basis for a technological society but because it is the most important intellectual institution with widespread impact on culture, politics and ideology...Universities assist in the creation and especially in dissemination of knowledge in societies where the "knowledge elite" is small".

George Thomas Kurian (1987) [3] said "Higher education represents an important form of investment in human capital that contributes to economic development by providing and enhancing skills, knowledge, and attitudes needed by high level professional, technical and managerial workers. Not only does higher education impart knowledge, but it also creates new knowledge through research and scientific and technological development, and thus universities and other higher education institutes made a two fold contribution to economy".

Transformation of education systems the world over is a continuous process. This transformation has been influenced by various factors like age, culture, religion etc. Similarly, education systems in India have seen many changes i.e., from Gurukul, Madarsa and Convent/ Public School education to the era of distance education and e-education. All these systems have been influenced by the cultures prevalent at that time. After Independence India inherited an educational system from the British, which failed to live up to our expectations in meeting the educational needs of all in India.

The distance education system has a wide scope for the emerging learning society in general and educationally underdeveloped or developing societies in particular. It has a message both for life long education as well as for universalisation of education. It is capable of acting as a useful medium for promoting diversified as well as vocational professional education. Distance education is source of inspiration for those who had 'dropped out' at some stage or other. In other words, distance education is an organized provision of learning opportunity on part time basis, outside the timetable of formal education system, covering a person's lifetime in his own environment, more or less according to his own perception and at his own time. The scope of distance education is very large as it is capable of serving vast and varied clientele.

Distance education is a potential medium and plays a vital role in training of manpower for different sectors like agriculture, health, literacy workers, computer literacy, and sex workers in developing countries. It is not possible for conventional education to train such a vast manpower due to its conservativeness and poor availability of resources with these nations.

WHAT IS DISTANCE/OPEN EDUCATION?

"Distance education is a systematically organized form of self study in which student counselling, the presentation of learning material and securing the supervising of the students success is carried out by a team of teachers, each of whom has responsibilities. It is made possible at a distance by means of media which can cover long distances; the opposite of distance education is direct education or face-to face . "A type of education that takes place with direct contact between lecturers and students". (Dohmen, 1967) [4].

Distance education according to Holemberg, (1981)[5] is a kind of education which, "covers the various forms of study at all levels which are not under the continuous, immediate supervision of tutors present with their students in lecture room or on the same premises, but which, nevertheless, benefit from the planning, guidance and tuition of a tutorial organization. According to Holmberg there are two basic elements of distance education.

These are: Separation of teacher and learner; and
Planning of an educational organisation.

Charles A.Wedemeyer (1977) [6] is the proponent of independent study. In his words "independent study consists of various forms of teaching – learning arrangements in which teachers and learners carry out their essential tasks and responsibilities apart from one another, communicating in variety of ways. Its purposes are to free on-campus or internal learners with the opportunity to continue learning in their own environment and developing in all learners the capacity to carry on self-directed learning, the ultimate maturity required of the educated person."

Otto Peters (1973)[7] describes distance education as an industrialized form of teaching and highlights its contemporary relevance. In his words "Distance teaching/education is a method of imparting knowledge, skills and attitudes which is rationalized by the application of division of labour and organizational principles as well as by the extensive use of technical media, especially for the purpose of reproducing high quality teaching material which makes it possible to instruct great numbers of students at the same time wherever they live. It is an industrialized form of teaching and learning".

According to Michael Moore (1973)[8] the distance education system departs from the conventional by mean of multimedia communication approach. "Distance teaching may be defined as the family of instructional methods in which teaching behaviours are executed apart from the learning behaviours, including those that in continuous situation would be performed in the learners presence, so that communication between the teacher and the learner must be facilitated by print, electronic, mechanical or other devices".

The system of distance education is more democratic and socialistic in nature in comparison to conventional system of education. It helps in diffusion of education and equalization of educational opportunities. Population in India is increasing rapidly and formal means of education have failed to keep pace with it. Besides this, existing educational resources are not being utilized for those to whom they are intended. Moreover, in a developing country like India, where a large number of people are deprived of educational opportunities due to poverty, distance education can serve as a mean for providing and equalizing educational opportunities by utilizing its multimedia approach.

HISTORY AND GROWTH OF DISTANCE EDUCATION IN INDIA

It is very difficult to trace the origin of correspondence education in the world. It came into being in several countries in different forms and at different times to meet the needs of those nations. Educational historians find that the idea originated in the 19th century when some European nations institutions were established to undertake coaching external students. Circumstances in different nations forced them to think for a viable alternative to provide education to those who are not able to make use of formal education system. It was during 1930 when correspondence education system made deep in roads in many nations. The founding of International Council of Correspondence Education[9] in 1930 is indicative of the fact that idea caught attention of educationists world over.

CORRESPONDENCE EDUCATION IN INDIA

Correspondence education in India came after Independence because of problems and limitations in formal education system. On the other hand, demand for education was increasing rapidly as it was perceived as a means of fulfilling economic necessities of life and achieving social status. Correspondence education was seen as an alternative medium of providing higher education to those who wish to improve their education further or was compelled to take employment or was not admitted in the regular stream.

The Planning Commission in its strategy stated "in addition to the provision in the Plan for expansion of facilities for higher education, proposals for evening colleges, correspondence courses and the award of external degrees are at present under consideration" Govt. of India, 1960[10]. On this basis, a proposal relating to correspondence courses was placed before the Central Advisory Board of Education (CABE) in its 20th meeting held in New Delhi on January 16-17, 1961. The CABE resolved that matter in detail be studied by a small committee before taking a policy decision in the matter. (Govt. of India, 1961)[11]. The Ministry of Education appointed an Expert Committee under the Chairmanship of Dr. D .S. Kothari, the then Chairman of UGC and other members from the UGC, the Ministry of Education and from the universities in India. The Committee made significant recommendations with regard of nature, scope and modes of organization of correspondence courses. (Govt. of India, 1962)[12]

In July 1962, University of Delhi for the first time established the Directorate of Correspondence Courses (later renamed as School of Correspondence and Continuing Education) on the basis of operational details worked out. In 1964, significantly Govt. of India appointed Education Commission to suggest a national pattern of education and on general principles and policies for the development of education at all stages and in all aspects. The Education Commission submitted its report in 1966 and made far-reaching recommendations about the reconstruction of education in India. The recommendation of Education Commission became the basis of the National Policy on Education formulated in 1968 and later also in 1986.

DISTANCE EDUCATION IN INDIA

In 1970, which was considered as International Education Year, the Ministry of Education and Social Welfare in collaboration with the Ministry of Information and Broadcasting, the University Grants Commission and the Indian National Commission for Cooperation with UNESCO, organised a seminar on the "Open University", which recommended for establishment of an Open University on an experimental basis. It was recommended in the seminar that a committee be appointed by the Govt. of India whether the outlined objectives can be achieved through open university and another problem related to the costs involved, formation of methods and media, categories of students to be served etc. Subsequently, Union Education Minister formed a Working

Group under the Chairmanship of Sh. G. Parthasarthi to consider the establishment of an open university in the country in (1971)[13]. The Group noted that the social and political awakening was spreading rapidly to the rural areas and advanced sections of the society, which has resulted in increased demand for higher education further resulting in establishment of institutions of higher learning. The working Group in its report stated:

"In a situation of this type, where the expansion of enrolment in higher education has to continue at a terrific pace and where available resources in terms of men and money are limited, the obvious solution, if proper standards are to be maintained and the demand for higher education from different sections of the people is to be met, is to adopt the Open University System with its provisions of higher education on part-time or own time basis. The Group, therefore, recommends that the Government of India should establish, as early as possible, a National Open University by an Act of Parliament."

The establishment of the first Open University in Britain in 1969 heavily influenced both the national seminar of 1970 as well as the 1982 UGC decision for establishment of a National Open University.

When the efforts were made to set a National Open University, the Govt. of Andhra Pradesh took concrete steps and appointed an Expert Committee to prepare a project proposal for starting an open university in the state. The Committee was asked to submit its report in 60 days. (Govt. of Andhra Pradesh, 1982)[14].

The Committee felt the need of alternative channels of education and Open University was the obvious choice. The Committee was of the firm opinion that the provision of access to higher education can be served by using multi-dimensional strategy. On the recommendations of the Expert Committee, the Govt. of Andhra Pradesh established the Andhra Pradesh Open University (now named as Dr. B.R. Ambedkar Open University) through an Act of Legislature in August, 1982 (Govt. of Andhra Pradesh, 1982)[15].

Encouraged by the success of establishment of an open university at state level, the Union Government also established Indira Gandhi National Open University* by an Act of Parliament on September 20, 1985. (IGNOU, 1985)[16].

The establishment of National Open University has been a welcome development because the impediments, which the traditional university system posed in the way of promoting distance education, could be surmounted.

Enthused by the success of distance education in the State of Andhra Pradesh and Indira Gandhi National Open University at national level, several State Governments also came forward with the idea of establishment of Open Universities in their States. As on date following nine State Governments have established open universities[17]:

(i) Bhim Rao Ambedkar Open University (BRAOU), Hyderabad (Andhra Pradesh, 1982)

(ii) Kota Open University (KOU), Kota (Rajasthan, 1987).

(iii) Nalanda Open University (NOU), Patna (Bihar, 1987).

(iv) Yashwantrao Chavan Maharashtra Open University (YCMOU), Nasik (Maharashtra, 1989).

(v) Raja Bhoj Open University (MPBOU), Bhopal (Madhya Pradesh, 1991).

(vi) Babasaheb Ambedkar Open University (BAOU), Ahmedabad (Gujarat, 1994).

(vii) Karnataka Open University (KSOU), Mysore (Karnataka, 1996).

(viii) Netaji Subhash Open University (NSOU), Kolkata (West Bengal, 1997)

(ix) Rajarishi Purshotam Das Tandon Open University, (UPTOU) Allahabad (U.P, 1999)

Other milestones in the field of open and distance education

---

* An overview of Indira Gandhi National Open University has been discussed in the forthcoming chapter (Chapter –II on pp. 27 to 36).

were establishment of Distance Education Council in 1991, Staff Training and Research Institute of Distance Education and upgradation of Electronic Media Production Centre as autonomous bodies under Indira Gandhi National Open University. Electronic Media Production Centre in IGNOU was made an autonomous body for synergisation of media related delivery systems also declared a nodal agency for the National Educational Channel "Gyan Darshan" launched by the Ministry of Human Resource Development to the advantage of distance education.

Enrolment in distance education in the country has been increasing regularly. Table 1 shows that, it was 64,210 in 1975-76 and increased to 28,61,628 in 2000-2001. The overall percentage of distance education in the country has increased from 2.58% in 1975-76 to 14.97% n 1998-99.

Table 1

Enrolment in Conventional Education and Distance Education in India from 1975-76 to 2000-2001

Year	*Enrolment in Colleges / Universities*	*Percentage of total enrolment*	*Enrolment in Corres-pondence/ Distance Education*	*Percentage of total enrolment*	*Total enrolment in higher education in India*
1975-76	2426109	97.42	64210	2.58	2490319
1976-77	2431563	96.83	79718	3.17	2511281
1977-78	2564972	95.56	119163	4.44	2684135
1978-79	2618228	95.15	133459	4.85	2751687
1979-80	2648579	95.09	136699	4.91	2785278
1980-81	2752437	94.30	166428	5.70	2918865
1981-82	2952066	93.84	193691	6.16	3145757
1982-83	3133093	94.07	197555	5.93	3330987

(Contd...)

1983-84	3307649	99.81	6231*	0.19	3313880
1984-85	3404096	99.46	18528*	0.54	3422624
1985-86	3605029	90.40	382719	9.60	3987288
1986-87	3757158	90.67	386536	9.33	4143694
1987-88	4020159	90.15	439168	9.85	4459327
1988-89	4285498	88.96	531991	11.04	4817489
1989-90	4602680	88.47	599706	11.53	5202386
1990-91	4924868	88.53	638231	11.47	5563099
1991-92	5265886	86.80	800594	13.20	6066480
1992-93	5534966	97.94	116417*	2.06	5651383
1993-94	5817249	97.16	169779*	2.84	5987028
1994-95	6113929	95.56	1031514	14.44	7145443
1995-96	6425624	88.23	857317	11.77	7300941
1996-97	6755455	87.49	965975	12.51	7721430
1997-98	7078214	86.52	1103024	13.48	8181238
1998-99	7417968⁺	85.03	1305875	14.97	8723843
1999-2000	n.a.	n.a.	2420838	n.a.	n.a.
2000-2001	n.a.	n.a.	2861628	n.a.	n.a.

Sources: Various UGC Annual Reports and Distance Education Council Reports, Manjulika Srivastava and Reddy V.V (2000) in *Distance Education in India: A Model for Developing Countries.*

⁺ As estimated by UGC.

Denotes enrolment in distance education only.

Table 2 provides the details of growth in number of open universities in the country, number of programmes offered by the open universities involving number of courses, student enrolment in each open university, number of Regional and Learner Support Centres in an university. Table 2 also indicates the number of academic counsellors, students passed, number of audio-video programmes produced and total number of personnel employed in these universities.

Importance of distance education in India in terms of increasing student enrolment indicates that the country is

Table 2

Growth and Status of Distance Education in India

Details of Information	*IGNOU*	*UPTOU*	*BRAOU*	*KOU*	*NSOU*	*YCMOU*	*MPBOU*	*BAOU*	*KSOU*	*NSOU*
Programmes on offer	50 *	30	21	21	9	54	29	9	23	3
Courses on offer	604	253	307	195	9	204	145	88	213	112
Student registered	196650	3307	93570	8141	1127	104551	56123	5556	27231	2126-
Student enrolment	561167	3307	318650	8793	-	397881	55912	24700	27231	-
Regional Centres	48	-	13	6	-	8	9	-	-	-
Study Centres	625	18	130	36	5	1399	670	46	30	36
Academic Counsellors	20000	-	4010	1000	48	4280	3140	694	2616	252
Students passed	53298	-	1897	1486	-	8224	3600	1017	2912	-
Audio Programmes	984	-	257	200	-	271	129	-	60	4
Video Programmes	941	-	198	11	-	153	16	-	42	-
Staff	1677	38	473	362	25	242	92	42	257	36

Source: Open Universities in India, Brief Information, Distance Education Council, IGNOU, 2000, p. 21.

poised to a new leap during the next two decades. India will expand substantially to meet the challenges of reskilling its population. The development of technologies and in particular telecommunication technology will bring in paradigm shift in programme delivery. The artificial cleavage between formal and distance education will reduce steadily. Though the way to knowledge driven economic progress through distance education appears to be more promising than ever before. The concern for quality of distance education programmes has to be maintained uniformly to avail maximum advantages of multiplier effect.

The quality of distance education* programmes depends upon the education system and its management. Management of any educational system is nothing but the adaptations of a coordinated approach of all the functions/sub-systems used for delivering the education to the learners enrolled for the purpose. The same principle also applies to the distance education system.

A systematic study of the management of distance education system in India will be certainly useful for delivering and implementing future distance education needs of the country. This study has been undertaken by the researcher to fill up the gap in area of the researches for management of distance education system in India.

To make a deeper study, Indira Gandhi National Open University, only one from the existing ten open universities presently functioning in India has been chosen. Another reason due to which Indira Gandhi National Open University has also been selected for the research/investigation to study Management of Distance Education System in India because it

---

* Distance Education System is not functioning well except in case of selected universities, which have been given resources by the Union and State Governments over the years. Most of the Distance education Institutes have been started without planning, without personnel and financial resources resulting into poor quality of services to the students and undue commercialization of distance education". (Dr.Hari Gautam, Chairman, UGC in his forward of "Distance Education in 21st Century" by Aruna and S.L.Goel (2000).

is not only the largest Open University in India, at the same time, it is also an apex body for promoting, disseminating, coordinating and maintenance of standards in distance education system in India. Indira Gandhi National Open University is also the 2nd largest Open University in the World after Central Broadcasting and Television University, Beijing.

In view of the above facts, researcher thought to conduct a comprehensive study to apprise the management of distance education system in India.

RESEARCH SCENARIO

Effectiveness of any system can be significantly measured by the level of job satisfaction of the personnel involved in its management and by the level of satisfaction of its clientele. Similarly, the level of morale and satisfaction of those involved in its management and day-to-day affairs and opinions of students about the satisfaction of the services provided to them in accordance with the provisions of the system can establish the effectiveness of the distance education system. This is only possible through the continuous feedback or research studies to keep the system effective as envisaged. Practically, the system of distance education is incomplete if provision for continuous feedback or research is missing or lacking, but it is also a fact that research is not inbuilt mechanism in the distance education system as has been rightly said by Murgatyard regarding the management of distance education; said that " most of research concerning management of administration of distance education is in descriptive, prescriptive and speculative or narrowly focused upon very small questions in the practice of management" American Journal of Distance Education (1989)[18]. He also observed " We lack a theoretical framework to provide our understanding of management challenges and skills and practices".

Distance education system has acquired the status of an important social organization after its fruitful existence of more than two decades since its evolution. It is making a valuable contribution in fulfilling the educational objectives of the society, with its advent as a viable supplement to the conventional education system. The attention of the world is drawn to the prospective academic implications. Here an attempt is made to give bird's eye view of the available literature in the field of distance education.

The International Scene

Scholars like Holemberg, Harry Hawkridge, Rumble, Perry, Kaye, Keegan, Daniel, Sewart, Moore, Peters come first among those who made a valuable contribution in the distance education and their studies have paved the way for many research programmes and projects in this area of education[19]. Their contribution in the field of distance education is invaluable. Many theories on the aspects of the use of multi-media, management of these institutes, the efficacy of student support services, the development of print media in distance education, propounded by these scholars have often been cited and approved at various platforms.

RESEARCHES IN INDIA

In India, systematic attempts to study various aspects of distance education begin in 1972 when Shashi (1972)[20] undertook the first research study on correspondence education. The researcher could identify 90 reputed comprehensive research studies in the area of distance education/correspondence education conducted so far. A detailed review of these studies indicates that they can be categorized into following nine different areas of distance education. These are summarized in Table 3.

Robinson (1989)[21] in her study on IGNOU conducted in the initial years rightly concluded that: "...The final challenges to IGNOU are related to those of degree validity and recognition and maintenance of academic standards.... The most realistic prognostication is that a dual system will continue to exist ......Questions must be raised, however, about the appropriateness of this model as a change agent and as an educational institution. Can a non-traditional innovative institution that operates independently from the traditional

Table 3
Area-Wise Research Studies Reported on Correspondence Education and Open Universities in India

Area	*Institutional projects*		*Private Projects*		*Master's Dissertations*		*M.Litt/M.Phil. Dissertations*		*Doctoral Dissertations*		*Total*
	CE	OU	CE	OU	CE	OU	CE	OU	CE	OU	
Concept Growth and Development	-	-	-	-	-	1	-	1	1	2	5
Curriculum/Course Planning and Development	-	2	-	1	-	-	2	-	-	2	7
Instruction/Teaching	-	-	1	7	-	-	1	1	-	1	11
Media and Technology	-	1	-	5	-	-	-	-	-	-	6
Learners and Learning	-	5	-	14	1	-	3	-	-	3	26
Institutional Policy and Management	1	-	-	-	-	-	1	-	1	1	4
Economics of Distance Education	-	4	6	-	-	-	-	-	-	-	10
Evaluation/Programme Evaluation	-	7	-	1	-	-	-	1	2	5	16
Staff Development	-	-	1	3	-	-	1	-	-	-	5
Total	1	19	8	31	1	1	8	3	4	14	90

system of higher education be a catalyst for change? Can it earn sufficient public, private enterprise and political support to be a change agent? Again, its success or failure will provide the answers to these questions..."

Table 3 clearly shows the marked absence of any research that addresses a fundamental question of managing such learning systems. The present research on Management of Distance Education system in India is an effort to fill this gap.

RESEARCH METHODOLOGY

Objectives of the Study

Main objective of this study is to apprise the Management of Distance Education System in India with specific reference to Indira Gandhi National Open University". The specific objectives of the study are as follows:

1. To identify different sub-systems (functions) involved in management of distance education.
2. To develop a conceptual model of management of distance education system.
3. To appraise the present practices (policies, procedures and approaches) adopted by Indira Gandhi National Open University for management of distance education in India against the conceptual model developed for the purpose.
4. To make suggestions in the existing management system of distance education adopted by Indira Gandhi National Open University.

The objectives of the study clearly indicate that the issues to be explored cover all aspects/elements of distance education system of Indira Gandhi National Open University. A review of literature on 'Research Studies in Distance Education in India clearly shows that management aspect is an area which is yet to be explored by the experts, administrators involved in distance education.

Analysis of the study are expected to provide a

comprehensive and critical examination of distance education system and also high light the micro aspects to enable the strengthening of the management of distance education system in general and the University in particular.

Research Design

The formidable problem that follows the task of defining the research problem is the preparation of the design of the research project, popularly known as "research design". +

The purpose of present work is to study and appraise sub-systems of management of distance education in India with specific reference to Indira Gandhi National Open University.

Major emphasize in the present research is on the discovery of ideas and insight with regard to management of distance education system. As the purpose of the study is to study different aspects of problem under study (Management of Distance Education System), therefore, the research design is used for the purpose is exploratory++ in nature.

Two methods+++ of exploratory research design (survey of

\+ "A research design is the arrangement of conditions for collection and analysis of data in a manner that aims to combine relevance to the research purpose with economy in procedure". (C.R. Kothari, Research Methodology (2000), P. 39).

++ "Exploratory research studies are also termed as formulative research studies. The main purpose of such studies is that of formulating a problem for more precise investigation or of developing the working hypothesis from an operational point of view. The major emphasize in such studies is on the discovery of ideas and insights. As such the research design appropriate for such studies must be flexible enough to provide opportunity for considering different aspect of a problem under study. Inbuilt flexibility in research design is needed because the research problem, broadly defined initially, is transformed into one with more precise meaning in exploratory studies, which fast may necessitate changes in research procedure for gathering relevant data". (C.R.Kothari, op.cite. P.117).

+++ "Generally, the following three methods in context of research design for exploratory studies are talked about: (a) the survey of concerning literature; (b) the experience survey and (c) an analysis of 'insight, stimulating' examples.

literature in the field of management of distance education system and the experience survey) have been used by the researcher to study the management of distance education system in India with reference to Indira Gandhi National Open University.

Survey of literature was done to formulate the research problem. It was helpful to the researcher not only to find out the gaps in the researches done earlier in the area of management of distance education system but it was also helpful to the researcher in identifying different sub-systems (functions) of management of distance education system and finally, in developing a Conceptual Model of Management of Distance Education System in India. During the research, existing secondary data available was also used for drawing inferences wherever required.

Next method used by the researcher was survey of people who have had practical experiences with regard to the management ot distance education system in India. The object of such survey was to obtain insight into the relationship between variables and new ideas relating to the research problem.

For the purpose of survey of experienced people, researcher has obtained information from teachers, academics, officers, coordinators/programme-incharge, those were involved in design, development, delivery and management of distance education in Indira Gandhi National Open University as well as the students, who were the end beneficiaries of the distance education system.

These categories of people were thought to be competent enough to contribute their ideas and opinions, towards the management of distance education system of IGNOU, were carefully selected as respondent to ensure representations of different types of experience. The respondent so selected then were interviewed (both by mail and in person) by the researcher. The researcher had prepared different sets of questionnaires for different categories of respondents.

Sampling

Sampling is the selection of a part of a group or an aggregate with a view to obtaining information about the whole. While choosing a sample, the population is assumed to be composed of individual units or members, some of which are included in the sample. Sample chosen must be representative of entire population. There are many advantages associated with the sampling i.e., less expensive, greater accuracy. The availability of a number of respondents in one place makes possible an economy of time and expense and provides a high proportion of usable responses. Properly constructed and administered questionnaire is most appropriate and useful data-gathering device[22].

As shown in the organizational chart of IGNOU in Chapter II, the University has nine Schools of Studies, ten Divisions, Electronic Media Production Centre, Staff Training and Research Institute of Distance Education and one Centre of Extension.

All nine divisions, Electronic Media Production Centre, Staff Training and Research Institute of Distance Education and 22 Regional Centres were selected for the purpose of study. Besides these, two out of nine Schools of Studies and 370 out of 615 Learner Support Centres were also included for the purpose of study. These two Schools, School of Management Studies and School of Computer and Information Sciences were purposefully included in the list as around 65% of the total students enrolment in the IGNOU was in the programmes of these two Schools at the time of study. (The study was conducted during academic session 2000). The reason for inclusion of 370 Learner Support Centres for the study was that these many centres were only activated for delivery of Computer and Management programmes of IGNOU.

All the teachers, and group 'A' officers in the School of Computers and Information Sciences (6 teachers and one group 'A' officer) and School of Management Studies (17 teachers and two group 'A' officers) were included for the purpose of getting their opinions as all of them were involved in design, development and management of programmes.

All group 'A' officers and academics (total 62) In all nine selected divisions of the University were surveyed as they were directly or indirectly involved or affect the different sub-systems of distance education and its management.

All the academics and group 'A' officers (totaling 100) working at 22 Regional Centres were also taken as a sample for the study as they were directly or indirectly involved in management, coordination and monitoring of Learner Support Centres.

All heads of 370 selected Learner Support Centres were also surveyed with the help of postal questionnaire to get their feedback towards management of support received from Regional Centres / University and delivery of support services to the students.

All the academics and group 'A' officers working in Electronic Media Production Centre (39) and in Staff Training and Research Institute of Distance Education (12) were also part of the study as they were also involved in management and delivery of media and training support, of IGNOU respectively.

Finally, 1200 out of 12,000 students who appeared in BCA & MCA of School of Computer and Information Sciences and Management Programmes of School of Management Studies in term-end examinations in December 2000 randomly selected students were mailed structured questionnaire. Out of which, 307 students had responded. Their opinions had been analyzed to apprise the management of distance education system in India.

The above categories of respondents were either responsible for design, development and management of different sub-systems of the University or were the end beneficiaries of the system of distance education.

Thus, following Table 4 depicts a detailed break up of the sample size of different constituents as defined above:

Table 4

No. of Respondents from Sampled Units

Sl. No.	*Name of Unit*	*Population Size*	*Sample Size*	*No. of Respondents*
1.	School of Management Studies	19	19	12
2.	School of Computer and Information Sciences	7	7	4
3.	Administration Division	11	11	6
4.	Academic Coordination Division	3	3	2
5.	Computer Division	7	7	5
6.	Finance and Accounts Division	10	10	7
7.	Library and Documentation Division	3	3	3
8.	Planning and Development Division	7	7	6
9.	Regional Services Division	7	7	6
10.	Student Registration and Evaluation Division	8	8	7
11.	Material Production and Distribution Division	6	6	5
12.	Staff Training and Research Institute of Distance Education	12	12	7
13.	Electronic Media Production Centre	39	39	10
14.	Regional Centres	100	100	55
15.	Learner Support Centres	370	370	105
16.	Students	12000	1200	307
	TOTAL			547

Efforts were made with the help of survey of 547 respondents to review the management of different sub-systems and their role in management of distance education system with reference to IGNOU.

Methods of Data Collection

"The task of data collection begins after a research problem has been defined and research design / plan chalked out".[23]

For carrying out systematic analysis of the management of distance education system in IGNOU, it was necessary that adequate information and opinion relating to different sub-systems (functions), their role, their interdependence and inter relation were available. For the purpose of collecting information and opinion, the researcher has carried out the research study through questioning technique.[+]

In order to collect information from different schools, divisions of IGNOU and to get the opinions of the selected respondents, 15 sets of structured non-disguised questionnaire were prepared for the different units of respondents.[++] By the help of these questionnaires, it was hoped to get useful data regarding management of distance education system with specific reference to IGNOU.

The questionnaires contained both types of questions i.e. open ended and closed. However, efforts were made to ensure that closed questions are in majority, as open- ended questions require more time in filling up of the questionnaire. Open-ended questions have been asked for ascertaining the view of respondents on policy matters, issues related to efficiency and effectiveness of services or provisions in the University.

Restricted or Closed questions have been used where only limited options are available to the respondents. In addition, tables have also been provided to the respondents to obtain the required data, which will be useful in making analysis of efficiency and effectiveness of the services offered by the University. Each questionnaire has been designed on the basis

---

+ The questionnaire method of collection of data was used of its versatility, speed and lesser cost. Moreover, the structured non-disguised questionnaire method was used in this investigation because it produces more relaxable data. Data obtained in structured non-disguised studies are easier to tabulate and interpret than data gathered other ways.

++ A common questionnaire was prepared for the respondents of Schools of Computer and Information Sciences and School of Management Studies.

of stated/ functional objective for each sub-system given in the profile of the University and on the systems process for accomplishment of stated/functional objectives for that sub-system. This shows that each questionnaire has two parts and the questions on systems process are common in the entire questionnaire except in the Students and Coordinators questionnaires. The questionnaire technique has been used mainly for securing the answers to a series of questions compiled systematically. Some of the sub-systems are responsible for setting the standards of quality in distance education system in the country, as University is also an apex body for promoting distance education in India. The questionnaires also made inquiry regarding management processes like planning, management, coordination, communication and control mechanisms etc., were also included in the questionnaire. The questionnaire for students included variables regarding the services provisioned and provided to them at the study/programme study centres to support their studies by using multi media approach *vis-à-vis* the opinion of students about the quality and effectiveness of these services and distance education system of the University.

Field Work

The main purpose of survey of selected respondents was to evaluate the management of distance education system in India with specific reference to IGNOU. For the purpose, the researcher visited two schools : (School of Management Studies and School of Computer and Information Sciences), nine divisions : (Administration, Finance and Accounts, Regional Services, Planning and Development, Student Registration and Evaluation, Material Production and Distribution, Library and Documentation, Academic Coordination and Computer Division, Electronic Media Production Centre and Staff Training and Research Institute of Distance Education and personally interviewed all the selected respondents (totaling 139) in these 13 sampled units. Out of these 80 teachers, academics and group 'A' officers only 58% were cooperative enough to the researcher to provide responses to the questions asked in the questionnaires. These responses were adequate enough to become ' STORE HOUSE' of information as regards the management of distance education system in IGNOU.

Further, data were also collected with the help of sending the questionnaire through mail+ to the outstation respondents (Regional Centres, Learner Support Centres and Students). The completed questionnaires were received back from 55 Regional Centres, 105 from Learner Support Centres and 307 from student respondents respectively.

In addition to above, the researcher to have his opinion also conducted an informal interview with the Vice-Chancellor of IGNOU on the issues like vision, long term and short objectives, planning, management, organizational structure, motivational factors, control mechanisms, technological up gradations of delivery services to its learners, status of research undertaken by the University on the various facets for strengthening distance education system.

DATA ANALYSIS

Basic assumptions underlying the study were that a sound management of distance education system does influence the performance of an Open University. An attempt had been made by the researcher to identify the forces, which were ineffective in making the distance education system successful.

In view of the nature of the study design, the techniques used for the analysis of management of distance education system were categorization, tabulations, frequency distribution, percentage, ranking method and charts.

+ The questionnaire was sent to the respondents in category of Regional Centre, Learner Support Centre and Students by mail, as the sample size of (1670 no.) was large enough and widely spread geographically. Moreover, such respondents were not easily approachable. Respondents were thought to be intelligent enough to give accurate responses to the questionnaires and they were given adequate time to send back the questionnaires. The response rate was about 33%, which was adequate enough to have the picture about the functioning of management system of distance education of IGNOU.

Findings are confined to factual reporting and are unembellished by the opinions of the researcher or by his prejudice. The data has been statistically analysed and presented in suitable tabular forms. Also the data obtained through open-ended questions and interviews are analysed content-wise.

LIMITATIONS OF THE STUDY

Every project has limitations. The present study like other research studies in similar and allied lines cannot claim to be a perfect one in all respects. Although, every effort was made to conduct the study as rigorously as possible, certain limitations were unavoidable, which are also indicated below:

1. It was not possible to cover the whole universe responsible for creation and maintenance of the distance education system and also that of IGNOU.
2. It was not possible to cover all the Students and Coordinators/Programme- In charge's of all the Study Centres of the university.
3. It was also not possible to cover all the teachers and officers working in all the Schools and Divisions of IGNOU.
4. This is the first study of its kind and no direction for the research was available.
5. Some element of bias on the part of respondents could not be altogether ruled out, although wherever possible checks were used to watch the correctness of the information.

Inspite of above mentioned limitations, in this present study, the researcher was confident that it would be sufficiently helpful in studying the management of distance education system with regard to IGNOU, identify the ineffective areas in different sub-systems/functions and would suggest relevant measures to make the system more effective so that higher education can be provided to each and everyone in India and literacy can be brought at par with the other developed countries of the world.

Chapter 2

INDIRA GANDHI NATIONAL OPEN UNIVERISTY: AN OVERVIEW

ESTABLISHMENT OF INDIRA GANDHI NATIONAL OPEN UNIVERSITY

Indira Gandhi National Open University[24] was established in 1985 by an Act of Parliament to democratize higher education in the country. The aim was to provide cost-effective, quality education to the large population including those living in remote and rural areas. Within 16 years after its inception, IGNOU has carved a niche for itself among the premier education institutions in the country.

The objectives of the University are following:

- To advance and disseminate learning and knowledge by a diversity of means
- To provide opportunities for higher education to a large segment of population
- To promote the educational well-being of the community in general
- To encourage the open university and distance education system in the country, and
- To coordinate and determine the standards in such systems

THE FUNCTIONS OF IGNOU[25]

The university has two major functions:

(i) Development and production of courses of delivery through the open learning and distance education system. It offers programmes of study leading to Degree, Diplomas, Certificates and like other institutions IGNOU is also engaged in research, training, and extension education activities, and

(ii) As an apex body, the University also acts as coordination and monitoring agency for the distance education system in the country. The Distance Education Council of the university has provided academic expertise, course material, training and financial support to State Open Universities.

FEATURES OF IGNOU

The main features of IGNOU are:

- national jurisdiction;
- flexible admission rules;
- individualized study: flexibility of place, pace and time of study;
- use of modern educational and communication technologies;
- student support services;
- cost-effective programmes;
- modular programmes;
- resource sharing, collaboration and networking with other Open Universities;
- comprehensive evaluation system;
- relevant programmes.

ORGANISATIONAL STRUCUTRE

The organizational structure[26] of Indira Gandhi National Open University is depicted in Figure 1 on next page.

Figure 1

ORGANISATIONAL STRUCTURE OF IGNOU

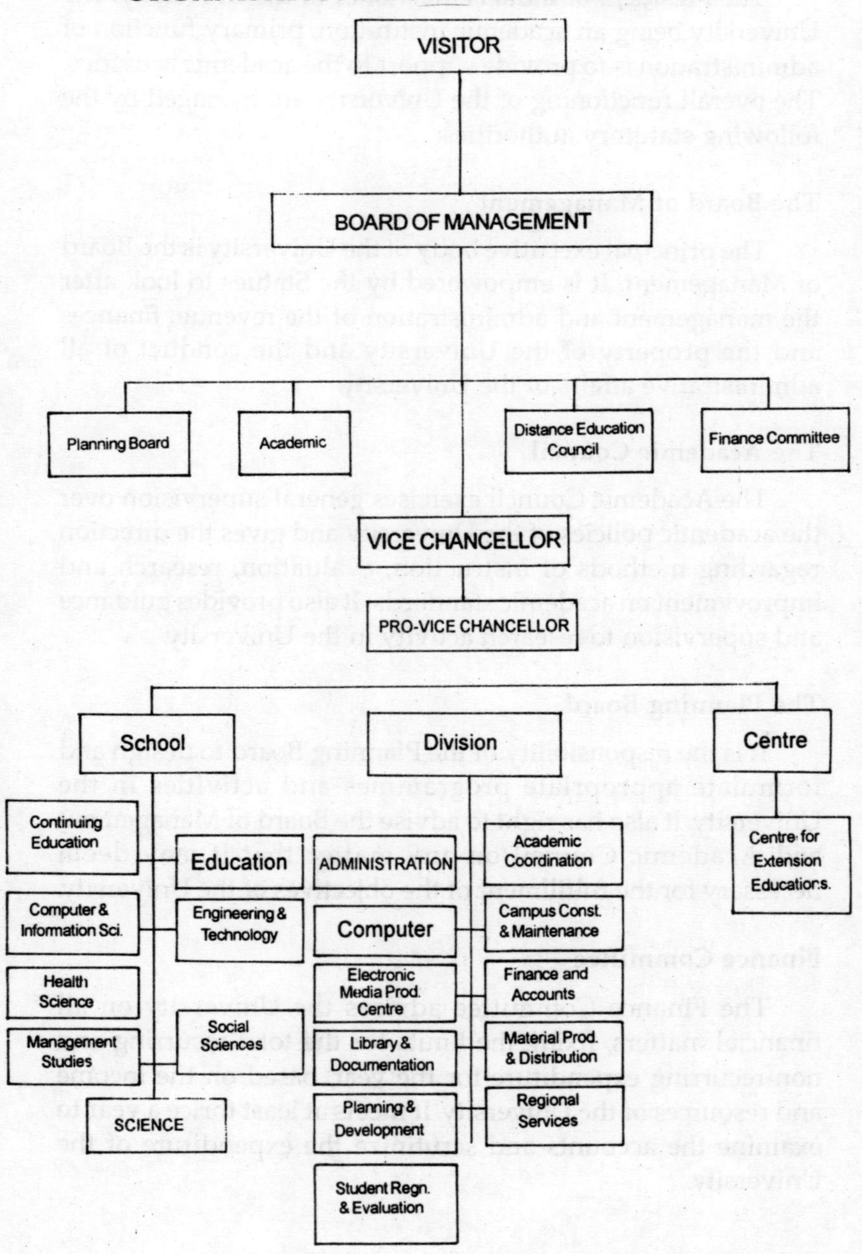

AUTHORITIES OF THE UNIVERSITY [27]

The President of India is the Visitor of the University. The University being an academic institution, primary function of administration is to provide support to the academic activities. The overall functioning of the University are managed by the following statutory authorities:

The Board of Management

The principal executive body of the University is the Board of Management. It is empowered by the Statues to look after the management and administration of the revenue, finances and the property of the University and the conduct of all administrative affairs of the University.

The Academic Council

The Academic Council exercises general supervision over the academic policies of the University and gives the direction regarding methods of instruction, evaluation, research and improvement on academic standards. It also provides guidance and supervision to research activity in the University.

The Planning Board

It is the responsibility of the Planning Board to design and formulate appropriate programmes and activities in the University. It also has right to advise the Board of Management and Academic Council on any matter that it may deem necessary for the fulfillment of the objectives of the University.

Finance Committee

The Finance Committee advises the University on all financial matters, fixing the limits for the total recurring and non-recurring expenditure for the year, based on the income and resources of the University. It meets at least thrice a year to examine the accounts and scrutinize the expenditure of the University.

The Distance Education Council

The University also functions as an apex body for the distance education system in the Country. The Distance Education Council established by the University for this purpose is entrusted with the primary responsibility of promoting and coordinating open learning and distance education system in the country, while monitoring and determining their standards. Major responsibilities assigned to Council are following:

- Promotion of Open and Distance Education System;
- Coordination of Distance and Open Education activities;
- Maintenance of Standards in Distance Education Institutions;
- Provision of Support to Distance Education Institutes and State Open Universities.

The officers of the University are Vice-Chancellor, Pro-Vice-Chancellors, Registrar, Directors, and Finance Officer. Vice-Chancellor is the ex-officio Chairman of the Board of Management, Academic Council, Planning Board, Distance Education Council, and Finance Committee. It shall be his/her duty to see that the Acts, the Statues, the Ordinances and Regulations are duly observed and have all the powers necessary to ensure such observance of all rules and regulations.

STUDENT ENROLMENT AT IGNOU

The university was established in 1985 but it actually started its functioning in the year 1987 with two programmes i.e., Diploma in Distance Education and Diploma in Management and there were only 4381 students in both these programmes. Thereafter, University has not looked back and has a phenomenal growth in the student enrolment. Table 5 shows the year wise registration of student till year 2001.

Table 5

Growth of Student Enrolment at IGNOU

Academic Year	*No. of Students Registered in the Year (0000's)*
1987	4.5
1988	16.81
1989	42.32
1990	48.28
1991	52.37
1992	62.37
1993	75.66
1994	84.18
1995	91.39
1996	130.22
1997	162.64
1998	163.39
1999	172.54
2000	196.65
2001	304.68

Source: Information Base, 2000, Student Registration and Evaluation Division and various Convocation Reports, IGNOU, New Delhi.

Table 6 indicates the programming-wise and School-wise break up during last five years. The highest growth is visible in programmes offered by School of Computer and Information Sciences. Programmes launched by the School of Continuing Education have not shown growth in student enrolment despite launch of many new programmes. The programmes launched by the School of Engineering and Technology are not picking up in terms of student enrolment. The enrolment is steadily increasing in programmes launched by the School of Education,

Table 6
Programme-wise and School-wise Enrolment of Students at IGNOU (1996-2001)

PROGRAMME	1996	1997	1998	1999	2000	2001
Certificates	11274	23587	26235	30029	32598	59363
Diploma	5276	11146	10964	8338	3346	4824
P.G. Diploma	4044	3358	3726	5992	5337	8713
Advance Diploma	-	-	32	9	676	2
Bachelors	35584	50655	61228	69594	83456	120993
Masters	66429	61216	50817	47793	60917	90298
Miscellaneous	7621	12683	10392	10793	10320	20206
TOTAL	130228	162645	163394	172548	196650	304681
SCHOOLS	1996	1997	1998	1999	2000	2001
Computers	14614	44162	57697	70888	94082	151859
Continuing Education	6791	5508	4816	6422	5752	8637
Education	1685	1199	1119	1631	3704	5029
Engg. & Technology	763	2220	1202	559	963	1513
Health Sciences	830	1086	1662	1764	1810	2659
Humanities	475	1067	1273	2221	1949	7815
Management	69504	65194	52274	43006	38623	46512
Social Sciences	31266	38259	38346	41105	44022	67990
Sciences	4140	3924	5005	4753	4764	6135
Miscellaneous	160	26	-	199	981	6532
TOTAL	130228	162245	163394	172548	196650	304681

Source: Convocation Reports of IGNOU and SR&E Division from 1996-2001.

Health Sciences and Humanities. Student enrolment has declined in programmes offered by School of Management Studies from 69504 in 1996 to 46512 in 2001. However, School of Social Sciences has maintained the growth in student enrolment, which is continuously increasing. There has been an increase in enrolment of students in arts, commerce, science, computer science, creative writing, journalism and engineering and technology programmes. Computer programmes have recorded a phenomenal increase due to the great demand world over.

Indira Gandhi National Open University during a short span of 16 years witnessed a phenomenal growth in terms of number of programmes, student enrolment, expansion of network of Regional and Study Centres. It has 64 programmes on offer and its student's enrolment has crossed over 5 million marks.

The University has not only witnessed growth in terms of student enrolment but in term of revenue collection also. Table 7 clearly shows the increase in revenue collection since its establishment in 1985.

It is true that revenue collection of University has ever been increasing since its inception and University is also witnessing the growth in terms of student enrolment and expansion in terms of number of programmes offered.

The data and facts shown in Table 5 to 7 presents a very rosy picture about the University, whereas there are lots of internal and external problems in the functioning of the University. A few incidents of managerial conflicts and poor student services were also reported in different newspapers and magazines. These problems also affect its delivery of student services, whether it is distribution of study material, audio video material, library books to the study centres, assignment evaluation and other facilities like counselling, audio-video counselling, teleconferencing and feedback on assignments to the students. Above all, this situation is due to lack of monitoring and control mechanisms for different sub-systems in the University. The expansion lacks proper planning, analysis of strength and weaknesses of the University.

Table 7

Revenue Collection in the University

Year	*Receipts+ during the year in Rs. Lac*	*Revenue Collection from Fees in Rs. Lac*	*Share of Fees in Total Receipts (in percentage)*
1989-90	2278.00	218.83	9.6
1990-91	2095.00	275.00	13.12
1991-92	2048.00	498.00	17.48
1992-93	2407.00	585.00	24.30
1993-94	2830.00	686.00	24.24
1994-95	3350.00	1259.00	37.58
1995-96	10749.00	1739.00	16.17
1996-97	6380.00	2590.00	40.59
1997-98	5640.00	2941.00	52.14
1998-99	8456.00	4407.00	52.11
1999-2000	13268.00	4806.00	36.22

Source: Information Base 2000, Student Registration and Evaluation, IGNOU, New Delhi and Annual Reports

It is essential for the efficient and effective operations of such a large magnitude that all management processes like planning, monitoring and coordination mechanisms are in place. The University possesses the best infrastructure and resources but has failed to utilize them for improving its services to the society at large. All the systems planned initially in the University are plagued with inefficiency, adhocism in absence of accountability. In absence of proper monitoring mechanisms

+ Receipts includes fees received from students, revenue from sale of forms, interest on bank deposits, miscellaneous receipts, grants carried forward from previous year, grants received from Government of India and grants received from State Governments.

delivery of student support services have become dysfunctional resulting in total anarchism in the University.

To be effective enough and provide quality in distance education, there is a need to follow management principles in all the functions of the university. The present research is an attempt by the researcher to apprise the management of distance education system with reference to Indira Gandhi National Open University.

Chapter 3

DISTANCE EDUCATION SYSTEM AND ITS MANAGEMENT

Distance education is one of the most rapidly growing areas in education and training today. Developments in communication and information technologies have significantly accelerated the pace of growth of distance education. Freedom from the constraints of time and space has provided an added incentive to large number of people, vastly heterogeneous in character and attitudes, to pursue different programmes of their choice to meet a variety of needs.[28]

The management of a dynamic distance education system has to grapple with a wide variety of issues and concerns. These include the mission and purpose of the system in the context in which it operates, the programmes and their curricula, the strategies for teaching and learning, the organisation of the infrastructure for communication and interaction with students, the choice of technology, policies regarding students and staff, the development and distribution of study materials, funding and the establishment of the credibility of the system itself.[29]

The managers of distance education systems have to address their tasks as the implementation of several integral components of a complex system. The ways in which decisions are taken and implemented in any of these components have a direct effect on all other components of the system. For instance, the choice of programmes will determine the systems of delivery and student assessment procedures; the enrolment levels will depend upon the managements' assessment of the market needs that influence the choice of programmes; the detailing of the curricula will influence the professional acceptance and recognition of the curricula will influence the professional acceptance and recognition of students produced by the programmes; the recruitment of staff and allocation of other resource have to be consistent with the objectives, structures and levels of each programme; the choice of media and technology support will have to be relevant to the needs of the programmes; and effective and efficient support systems have to be in place.[30]

Distance education is an enterprise and exhibiting industrial features, use of management techniques are much more appropriate. Distance education should be managed as system because of use of all human and technological resources are planned, it also has sub systems within the system, the most important of which are the design sub systems and those for instruction and learner support, evaluation and production. Management of such an institution requires interdependent sub-system, which involves constant administrative attention and teamwork. The management of distance teaching university involves four key elements *i.e.*, planning, organization, implementation and controlling (Cole, 1993)[31] Thus tutoring is not a management function, but almost every other non-routine task, which leads to successful learning, has a management aspect.

Thus, the success of quality education initiative is greatly dependent on the managerial factor. It is essential that the top management of any learning system is completely committed to the concept and cause, and is able to visualize the future as a whole and take appropriate decisions. This means that mission of the educational institute has to be clearly defined, its long and short term objectives are clearly identified, strategies, coordination mechanism, financial provisions are accordingly planned.

Distance Education as a System

The Open University as an organisation, that has several

sub-systems[32], which include:

- Strategic planning and resource management;
- Prescribing the courses, determining the curricula and multi-media, setting the standards of achievement for students;
- Research for system development and programme evaluation;
- Administering the organisation, procurement of stores, equipment, books;
- Recruiting teachers, administrators, technocrats and support staff and training them and administering their conditions of service;
- Construction and maintenance of buildings, staff houses etc;
- Admitting students, collecting fees, maintaining records;
- Management of database systems;
- Providing learner support services like print material, media and technology support, library facilities, counselling, practical, feedback on assignments etc.
- Holding examinations and certifying the performance of students;

The above activities within the context of an open university, each of the above set of functions, or sub-systems, has no independent existence or goals. Courses have to be prescribed to enroll students, teachers have to be appointed to teach the students, examinations have to be held to test their performance and award degrees, and each of these functions should inform the other for achieving the university's goals of educating people. In order to ensure that all this happens in an orderly manner, each of these functional areas has to be structured with its roles, responsibilities and relationships with each other clearly defined, and the methods and processes of interaction among them specified through appropriate procedures.[33]

People who constitute them define organisations, at their core. They are therefore part of the social systems, which constantly interact with their environment. They are also known as open systems, which in a larger context are sub-systems of the environment within which they operate. The environment itself consists of social, economic, political and legal sub-systems. In the university, how the environment influences the determination of policies, courses, admission procedures and so on from time to time. The national policies that guide the education system would determine the university policies with regard to admission of students and appointment of teachers (equal opportunities, special provisions for the disadvantaged sections, remedial programmes for the weaker students); induction of new technologies would influence determination of course content (communication technologies, computer applications); and funding regimes would affect the scales of fees charged for different programmes.[34]

Systems Approach

A systems approach to the problem means that a piecemeal approach is replaced by an overall approach. A systems approach enables us to design complex systems by the efficient use of resources in the form of men, money, machine and materials, so that the individual sub-systems making up the total system may be designed, fitted together, checked and operated to achieve the stated goals in the most efficient way. Four different names *viz.*, Systems Engineering, Systems Analysis, Systems Approach and Operational Research, are used to explain this methodology (systems approach). Jenkins (1969)[35] says, "systems engineering is concerned with placing a big emphasis on the design of the total system and not individual sub-systems".

Dearden (1972)[36] says, "The systems approach is nothing more or less than what a competent, smart, adequate business executive adopts in the ordinary conduct of his business".

Makridakis (1971)[37] says, "the systems approach to management is basically a way of thinking. The organisation is viewed as an integrated complex of interdependent parts which are capable of sensitive and accurate interaction among themselves and with their environment." Forester (1961)[38] considers the systems approach as, "interconnections, the compatibility, the effect of one upon other, the objectives of the whole, the relationship of the system to the users and the economic feasibility" more than the parts standing in isolation or the functional components.

A system operates through its components, which complement and supplement the operations of each other. The systems approach needs to be applied in design of total system and also to each sub-system. Its each sub-system needs to be structured carefully to include the steps described in systems approach, and integrated into the total educational system. A system[39] has following components:

- A number of parts or sub-systems which put together in specific manner form the whole system;
- Boundaries in which each part exists;
- A specific goal or goals expressed in terms of performing a task, producing an output or providing a service etc; and
- Close inter-relationship and interdependence among the different sub-systems.

Inter-relationship among the sub-systems can be identified in the following terms:

- The flows which exist between them, such as the flow of communication;
- The structure within which they relate to each other;
- The feedback and the control process and mechanisms, which exist to ensure that the system is moving towards the desired objectives.

CONCEPTUAL MODEL OF MANAGEMENT OF DISTANCE EDUCATION SYSTEM

A review of three existing literature on distance education (Systems model of Distance Education, Holistic model of Distance Education, Transactional model of Distance Education) depicts different sub-systems of distance education and its interaction. Success of Open learning initiatives (Distance Education Programmes) seldom happen by chance, they are dependent upon management on planning+, organising*, implementing# (motivating and leading), and controlling$.

+ **Planning:** Planning is the most basic and pervasive process involved in managing. It means deciding in advance what actions to take and when and how to take them. Planning is required for allocation of resources towards achieving its objectives in the best possible manner, as they are limited. Secondly, planning is for anticipating the future opportunities and problems.
Planning involves organisational identity, sense of purpose and response to new opportunities. Studies of organisational structure and design need to examine the 'environmental fit'.

* **Organising:** The formal grouping of activities and people to facilitate achievement of objectives is organising. The type of issues it involves is organisational structure, degree of decentralization, and levels of management, span of control, delegation of authority, unity of command, staffing and line and staff relationships.

Implementing: After having established plans, and appropriate structure to achieve the set objectives of the organisation, implementation of programmes and plans are essential to achieve the objectives of the organisation by canalization of the behaviour and actions of individuals towards achievement of objectives. It also includes leading which means inspiring and influencing towards achieving the organisational objectives. Leader has to be objective in his judgments and decisions and interest of his people / team may be paramount importance to him. Leader should be able to mould himself according to the unique situational requirements.

$ **Controlling:** Planning and controlling go hand in hand. There cannot be any control without a plan and plan cannot be successfully implemented in the absence of control. Controls provide a means of checking the progress of the plans and correcting any deviations that may occur along the way. A control is meaningful only when there is clear-cut responsibility for activities and results. It is meaningless to have a control process, which simply points out deviations but cannot pinpoint the area in which they occurred and who is responsible for

These four important functions of management offer a framework within which all open learning systems must function.

Management is about directing the energies and resources of organisations to purposeful, coordinated and goal-oriented activities. The functions of managers include planning, organising, implementing and controlling. These managerial functions are essentially the same regardless of the type of the organisation, or the level of the managers in the organisation. The Vice-Chancellor of a University, the Dean of a Faculty or the Registrar performs these functions in the same manner, as does the President of a manufacturing company, the Marketing Manager of its products or the Secretary of the company.

The researcher has designed a conceptual model for management of distance education system+ (see Figure 2). This model has been designed on the basis of amalgamation of managerial functions (planning, organising, implementing and controlling) and different sub-systems of distance education. The suggested framework for management of distance education system attempts to organise the vast amount of information that relates directly or indirectly to the proper management of distance education system by an Open University. It depicts a closed loop system consisting of sub-systems such as formulation of strategic plans and management of resources, management of academic activities (print and media), management of administrative activities, management of learner support services, management of database management systems. As such, this model portrays the relationships between all the major activities of any Distance Education System and its managerial implications.

---

taking corrective measures. Controls may be used to measure physical quantities, monetary results or to evaluate intangibles such as employee morale, loyalty.

\+ This conceptual model has been designed after the study of three existing models of distance education; these are : (i) Systems model of Distance Education by Greville Rumble, (ii) Holistic model of Distance Education by Perraton, H. and (iii) Transactional model of Distance Education Henir, F. and Kaye, A. They are depicted in Exhibit II (A-C).

Figure 2

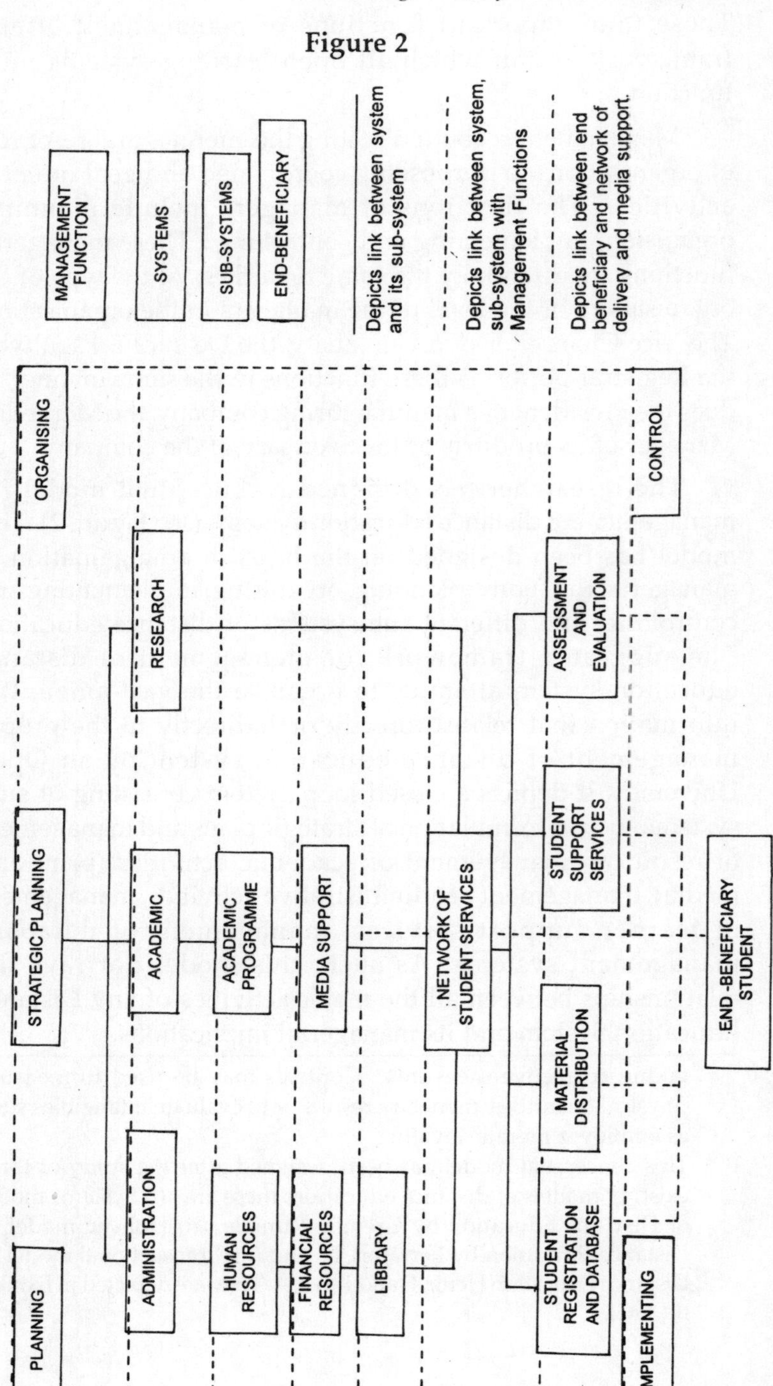
CONCEPTUAL MODEL OF MANAGEMENT OF DISTANCE EDUCATION SYSTEM.
MANAGEMENT FUNCTION
SYSTEMS
SUB-SYSTEMS
END-BENEFICIARY
Depicts link between system and its sub-system
Depicts link between system, sub-system with Management Functions
Depicts link between end beneficiary and network of delivery and media support.
PLANNING
STRATEGIC PLANNING
ORGANISING
ADMINISTRATION
ACADEMIC
RESEARCH
HUMAN RESOURCES
ACADEMIC PROGRAMME
FINANCIAL RESOURCES
MEDIA SUPPORT
LIBRARY
NETWORK OF STUDENT SERVICES
STUDENT REGISTRATION AND DATABASE
MATERIAL DISTRIBUTION
STUDENT SUPPORT SERVICES
ASSESSMENT AND EVALUATION
IMPLEMENTING
END-BENEFICIARY STUDENT
CONTROL

Chapter 4

STRATEGIC PLANING AT IGNOU

Strategic Planning[+] is the elaboration of the grand design for accomplishing any mission. It is a major management tool, which helps institutions/organizations achieve their objectives. Strategies outline how the given objectives are translated into realities. In order to meet these objectives, it is essential to draw plan of action for the management of the system, what is to be done, how to be done and at what cost. This detailed exercise is done to meet the long-term and short-term plans. These planned objectives from the management's point of view are called goals, which are set in the context of environment in which the system has to exist [40].

The process of strategic planning helps management at regular intervals to review the plans already prepared, make necessary modifications considering the changes in the environment and finally review the actual achievements against the target to ensure efficiency. [41]

Planning is the core of management functions, which helps an institution in its survival and growth in a changing environment.

Planning is essentially a blue print for action, for achieving

---

+ Strategic Planning is intelligence design choice activity concerned with defining the firm's basic characteristics, the composition of its business mix, quantitative and qualitative projection of its attainment and developing strategies for the organization as a whole as well as for different critical functions. (R.M. Srivastava and Divya Nigam, Corporate Strategic Management, Pragati Prakashan, Meerut, 2000, p.9)

a mission. A plan sets out the activities systematically so that shared objectives can be achieved.

For management of distance education system, it is essential to draw a plan of action spelling out the strategy for its accomplishment and the costs involved. These plans can be termed as goals from the management's perspective set in the context of environment in that the system has to exist.

In distance education system, planning can be helpful in evolving various systems/components like objectives of the institution, the programmes and curricula it will develop and how; what kind of strategies will be used in transaction of teaching learning process; what will be its personnel policy; how resource mobilization will be done; and what kind of monitoring and evaluation systems will be needed for this purpose.[42]

STRATEGIC PLANNING AT IGNOU

Planning and Development Division of IGNOU[43] is responsible for framing policies and strategic plans for making the Open Learning System contextual and relevant. The objectives of this division as given in the IGNOU profile (2000) are as follows:

- to set the vision and direction for the open and distance learning system;
- to optimize the utilization of national resources for the Open Learning System;
- to set short and long term goals for the growth of the University and;
- to install Total Quality Management in all the areas of the operations of the University;

The Vision of IGNOU

The vision+ of the institution is how it would like to be and

+ **Vision** of an organization has a very long-term orientation and is devised from organization philosophy. **Vision** represents a

mission has to be compatible with its vision, it then sets its broad objectives and those are to be transformed into specific attainable objectives"[44]. The objective or mission* of the organization is a critical factor, which influences its design. In a way, organizations objectives determine which particular segment of the environment it is prepared to interact with. A clear statement and understanding of an organizations mission or objective has a critical influence on its functioning [45].

Respondents from Planning and Development Division of IGNOU on inquiry regarding the vision revealed that University has not yet laid down any vision and mission for itself. However, following objectives were formulated as back as in 1985. They are:

- To advance and disseminate learning and knowledge through a diversity of means, including communication technology;
- To provide opportunities for higher education to a large segment of the population;
- To promote the well being of the community;
- To encourage the Open University and distance education system in the educational pattern of the country.

It is suggested that university should devise vision/mission for the university and policies should be formulated accordingly. The vision for the university may be defined as:

---

challenging portrait of what the organization and its members can be in the future. Therefore, organization should create projections about where it should go and what major changes lie ahead. (L. M. Prasad, 2001, Human Resource Management, S.Chand and sons, New Delhi p.87)

* **Mission:** An organization establishes mission by defining the basic purpose of its existence and how it justifies its existence. It has to define the business it is in, the market it tries to serve, and the types of outcomes. In contrast to vision, is more discipline and less future oriented. It is still broad and needs to be converted to goals to become operational and useful. (L. M. Prasad, 2001 Op.Cit. p.87)

"To endeavour for national development and global progression by providing relevant and qualitative education through convergence of educational systems and technologies".

To have effective strategic planning and management of system, the following mission statement has been proposed by the researcher:

"To accelerate the process of furtherance of comprehension, theoretical and practical both. To unwrap new vistas of knowledge and help the students in augmentation of vision, and engendering catholicity of views."

Policy Formulation Mechanism in the University

Policy+ might be defined as basic statement serving as guide for administrative action.[46]

Respondents from Planning and Development Division have stated that policies in the university are formulated through various bodies like Academic Council, School Boards, Finance Committee, Distance Education Council and Planning Board, and finally approved by the Board of Management, whose Chairman is the Vice-Chancellor.

The policy formulation mechanism in the university should be on the basis of inputs received from different Schools and Divisions. Inputs received from Schools and Divisions should be the basis for short term and long-term plans of the university. These short-term and long-term plans should be based on the objectives of the university laid down by the Act of Parliament. Planning Board of the University is responsible to design and formulate appropriate programmes and activities in the

---

\+ Policy is a general statement or understanding, which provides guidelines for decision making to managers in respect to various functions and activities. The organization is required to formulate policies in different areas, which are necessary for achieving organization goals. The policies may be required for various functional areas to guide as to how these functions can be performed and how these functions interact among themselves and with their relevant external environment. (L.M.Prasad 2001, Human Resource Management, Op.cit. p.87)

University. It has the right to advice the Board of Management and Academic Council on any matter that it may deem necessary for the fulfillment of the objectives of the University.

Director, Planning and Development Division is a member of the Planning Board of the University and division also acts as a secretariat and provide inputs about the planning of academic programmes, student services, management of resources, five year plans and Annual Report to the Planning Board. This indicates that Planning and Development Division can play an important role in planning, policy designing and development, short-term plans, long-term plans, resource mobilization and in strengthening the different sub-systems of the university by implementing the management information systems in the university and also by ensuring its adherence by all the sub-systems. Monitoring of implementation of plans should be a continuous process and corrective measures as and when needed, should also be taken for achieving the planned targets.

Long-Term Growth Plans of the University

Planning[+] for a long duration like, five-year plans are termed as Long-term plans of the University. Long-term plans of an institution contain inputs from various departments in the university. Long-term plans of university provide a direction for next five years to the university.

The Planning and Development Division prepares long-term plans for the university. The objectives of long-term planning of the University as opined by respondents are:

[+] Planning is the systematic development of activities aimed at reaching agreed objectives, by a process of analyzing and selecting from among the various strategies and opportunities that have been identified as being available. It is regarded as a rational process that is comprehensive in its scope and leads to results, but it is bedvilled by the irrational unthoughtout policy statements flashes of inspiration, or sudden decisions to change well established ground rules, it is often far from comprehensive; and it may lead to nothing. (Greville Rumble, 1986, The Planning and Management of Distance Education, Croom Helm, London and Sydney)

- To make full use of technology for improving the delivery of student services;
- To promote vocational and professional programmes;
- To arrest drop-out rate and increase the number of successful students;
- Quantification of long -term plans in terms of student number, academic programmes and extension activities. This could be to develop a system for mass training and education, teaching through resource based learning and networked education system.

Long-term plans of the University are vague and fail to quantify the targets *i.e.*, number of programmes to be launched during next five years, student enrolment during next five years, likely revenue generation and its utilization during next five years, utilization of surplus funds generated, and further how to meet the shortfall in revenue collection should form part of the five year plans of the university.

Long-term plans should also address innovative and technology up gradation measures for next five years. The long-term plans of the university fail in spelling out the strategies to achieve the laid down objectives.

The powers are centralized in the Vice-Chancellor who keeps on changing during plan periods and priorities are redefined. The targets are reset. Above all, strategies for accomplishment of plans are not properly designed. This situation does not allow achievement of objectives of the long-term planning. Similarly, short-term plans of the university are annual plans and they should be phased plans of the long-term plans of the university, which is missing.

To find out the nature of planning and its different features at IGNOU, opinions were also obtained from the respondents of two Schools, nine Divisions, Staff Training and Research

---

+ Planning includes defining goals, establishing strategy, and developing plans to coordinate activities. (Stephen.B.Robbins, 1998, Organizational Behaviour, Prentice Hall of India (P) Ltd, New Delhi, P.3)

Institute of Distance Education and Electronic Media Production Centre and 22 Regional Centres. Their perceptions about different features of planning are depicted in Table 8.

Table 8
Nature of Planning at IGNOU+

Nature of Planning	*No. of Respondents*			
	Yes	*No*	*No Response*	*Total*
Planning as a regular feature	107(79.26)	8(5.93)	20(14.81)	135
Flexibility in planning to enable corrective measures	105(77.78)	17(12.59)	13(9.63)	135
System of integrated planning	89(65.93)	37(27.41)	9(6.67)	135
Control mechanisms for timely achievement of plans	85(62.96)	34(25.19)	16(11.85)	135
Appropriateness of organizational structure for achievement of objectives	89(65.93)	37(27.41)	9(6.67)	135
Responsibilities are logically structured for achievement of plans	92(68.15)	31(22.96)	12(8.89)	135
Communication system for achievement of plans	79(58.52)	50(37.04)	6(4.44)	135
Planning for flawless and uninterrupted development and delivery	85(62.96)	34(25.19)	16(11.85)	135
Monitoring of Plans	92(68.15)	31(22.96)	12(8.89)	135

Source: The responses of the respondents from Schools, Divisions, STRIDE, EMPC and Regional Centres.

(Figures in brackets are the percentage of the total)

To be effective enough, planning system of any open university must be a regular feature. As shown in the Table 8, 79.26% respondents feel that planning of activities is a regular feature in the university system. A small number of respondents were of the opinion that planning was not a regular feature and activities were not properly planned.

Planning should have built in flexibility because circumstances often change. Planning to be useful must be both stable and reasonably flexible. 77.78% respondents in Table 8 believe that planning in the university is flexible enough to take corrective measures, if situation demands. The main quality of a good plan is its inbuilt flexibility to accommodate the changes if circumstances demand.

Out of 135 respondents from the university, majority of 65.93% respondents feel that there exists the system of integrated planning for attaining the objectives of the university, 27.41% do not find the system of integrated planning and 6.67% are silent on this aspect.

From Table 8, it is also clear that majority of 62.96% respondents feel that there are control+ mechanisms for timely achievement of plans. According to them, control mechanisms are an inbuilt part of plans, whereas 25.19% respondents do not feel having adequate control mechanisms for timely achievement of plans in the university.

Respondents by majority of 65.93% feel that organizational structure of the university is appropriate enough for achieving the laid down objectives of the university whereas 27.41% respondents do not find the organization structure appropriate for achievement of objectives of the university. Organizational structure of a distance education institute should facilitate planning and management of the objectives of distance education. Organizational structure also results in improved coordination among different sub-systems of the distance education system. The organizational structure is not a stable phenomenon; organization structure is influenced by the growth and development, decentralization and centralization of authority.

The University is also an apex body for promoting, monitoring and maintenance of standards in distance education

---

+ Controlling is monitoring of activities to ensure that they are being accomplished as planned and correcting any significant deviation. (Stephen, B. Robbins, Op.Cite, p3.)

system in the country, like that of University Grants Commission for conventional education. This aspect has to be borne in mind while designing the organizational structure. Therefore, it is suggested that Distance Education Council should be put on the top of the structure so that it is possible to plan the distance education system strategically *vis-à-vis* resource management and to put control mechanisms for maintenance of standards on the basis of performance indicators designed for each aspect of distance education system. This will also result in cost-effectiveness since presently resources of States and Centre both are utilized for the same purpose *i.e.*, duplication of efforts and resources.

Finally, the organizational structure should also facilitate decision making process in the university, should facilitate management of network of learner support services which includes admission processes, examinations processes, material distribution system, delivery of audio-video systems in the organization. Still, organization of distance education system is based on functional divisions. Flat organizational structures are preferred by professionally managed institutions as they help in cutting the channels and are less time consuming, efficient and cost-efficient.

92 respondents from Schools, Divisions, STRIDE, EMPC and Regional Centres are of the opinion that responsibilities are logically structured and sharply defined for achievement of plans. However, 31 respondents do not find the responsibilities logically structured for achievement of plans. The clearly defined responsibilities result in better productivity, efficiency, team spirit, and cohesiveness in the organization. This will have further implications on the delivery of student services, in terms of delivery of study material in time, improved quality of counselling and timely feedback on assignments and timely receipts of results/grade cards. This shows that logical structuring results in improvement of functioning in the whole chain or system of activities. Therefore, it is suggested that job specification, control mechanisms, responsibilities for all the cadres in the university are put in

place. This will also help in bringing cohesiveness and team spirit among the officers and staff. Clarity in roles and responsibilities will also result in more productivity and quality of services and maintenance of standards in the system.

Effective communication system is necessary to keep all the levels of personnel in the organization abreast of the developments in the institution that perfect them for facilitating the achievement of plans in the open university system.

As shown in the Table 8, 58.52% respondents feel that communication system facilitates timely achievement of plans/ targets in the university, 37.04% respondents feel that communication systems in the university are not effective to achieve the targets of university in time and 4.44% are silent on this aspect. The communication system plays a vital role in distance education system. It is the effectiveness of communication, which makes one aware about certain activity, function, and objectives. The communication should be clear, easy to understand and in time. Clarity in communications makes people understand the purpose of communication. The communication should be in a simple language and words, which are easy to comprehend, and do not result in confusion to the receiver. The communication should be in time so that it results in timely completion of plans/targets in the university. Though majority feels that communication systems in the university facilitates timely achievement of plans but it is also correct that study material is delayed, feedback on assignments is delayed, and audio-video support is missing from the system and so on as opined by Students. This all shows that communication among sub systems of the university and to the end user *i.e.* student is not effective. The distance education system is primarily based on the principles of effective communication. Therefore, it is must that communication system is always kept effective so that it results in timely achievement of plans in different systems in the university and benefits to the end beneficiary.

Majority of 62.96% respondents feel that planning is done to ensure flawless and uninterrupted development and delivery, however, 25.19% respondents do not feel so. The difference of opinion among the respondents on planning of flawless and uninterrupted development and delivery of the programme indicates that defined procedures for planning are either not followed or are bypassed to cut short. While analyzing the responses of the respondents in Planning and Development Division it is not difficult to infer that planning systems are not in proper shape. Therefore, it is suggested that due care should be taken to ensure that planning for programme development is flawless and uninterrupted.

Monitoring of implementation of plans is also essential to ensure that targets are achieved in time without making any compromise with the quality of produce or services. Henry Fayol (1949)[47] says, "in an undertaking, control consists in verifying whether everything occurs in conformity with the plans adopted, the instructions issued, and the principles established. Its object is to point out weaknesses and errors in order to rectify them and prevent recurrence. It operates on everything- people, things and actions".

68.15% respondents in Table 8 feel that implementation of plans are continuously monitored in the university whereas, 22.96% respondents do not find monitoring as a system in the university. Students responses, in Table 12, 14, 17 and 20 towards library facilities, audio-video and teleconferencing facilities, delivery of study material and assignments and timely feedback on assignments respectively, clearly indicate that organization of activities are not continuously monitored in the university. The university has totally failed in taking appropriate remedial measures for ensuring timely and quality services to its students, which is its sole objective. Efficiency and effectiveness of its sub-systems can be solely judged by the student's satisfaction while studying in the university. Therefore, University should implement control mechanisms and introduce quality maintenance measures in each system, aimed at providing delivery of student services. The monitoring reports should be discussed at appropriate platforms and remedial actions should be taken to check the shortfalls, deviations and quality of services as provisioned for students must be ensured.

Despite the fact that majority of respondents in Table 8 have opined that planning is a regular feature, there exists flexibility in planning and system of integrated planning, organization structure is appropriate for achievement of objectives, responsibilities are logically structured, there exists effective communication system in the university, planning is flawless and uninterrupted and monitoring of implementation of plans is a systematic process, the students by majority have categorically denied receipt of timely and quality of student support services from the university.

Therefore, finally it is suggested that university should review its planning process, organization of activities, implementation of plans and above all ensure that control mechanisms provide immediate and instant information about the delay in timely accomplishment of targets. Coordination among sub-systems of the university has to be very-very effective as distance education system is a complex and industrialized form of educational system. To achieve greater efficiency in its coordination system, the prerequisite is timely, appropriate and clear communication among the sub-systems of the university and with the students. Simultaneously, university should also undertake organizational restructuring commensurate to its phenomenal growth since coordination in its activities on such a larger scale is becoming difficult. Further decentralization and delegation of all activities aimed at student services to its Regional Centres appears to be need of the hour.

Suggestions for the Improved Performance of Strategic Planning at IGNOU

Forward planning as a management tool has not yet captured the imagination of academics in distance education though, there is an assured high potential market for this system and still there is no major competition. Distance education system has to create market, gain creditability and acceptance among the public. The processes in distance education are much more complex, being the combination of several processes/ operations like an industry. The processes in distance education thus need greater degree of efficiency, accuracy in organization and scheduling of various functions within the constraints of time. Planning is the established management tool for this purpose and more so in the distance education. Corollary, foregoing discussions, the researcher has proposed following suggestions to improve strategic planning at IGNOU:

- There should be flow of information among academics; independent work by the academics should be encouraged. Functional autonomy to a degree should be allowed encouraging participative and teamwork in the functioning.
- The flow of information among the academics of the division needs strengthening.
- Planning and Development Division should be under direct control of the Vice-Chancellor and planning process should encourage better coordination between IGNOU –SOU in programme development and implementation.
- Communication system within the division and Schools of the university should be strengthened providing transparency, accountability and respectability towards various functions and effective Management Information System.
- Flow of data of all kinds to the division should be made compulsory. Each officer/academic of the division should be allotted some School/Divisions for monitoring.

To appreciate above suggestions in proper perspective, it is necessary to admit that University is not functioning on the principles of management. The system of planning, organizing, implementation and control mechanism does not exist, resulting in adhocism and lack of coordination among its various sub-systems. Unless all the systems are allowed to work independently and efficiently in a planned and organized manner, implementation and control mechanisms are strengthened, it will be very difficult to provide, quality student services timely, which is the main objective set out by the Parliament for the University.

Chapter 5

MANAGEMENT OF ADMINISTRATIVE SYSTEM AT IGNOU

Administration+ plays a crucial role in providing functions and systems support to the organization and all communication among sub-systems. The concept of administration is associated with the exercise of power and authority under rules, regulations and procedures and exercises control over the administration of personnel and finance.

The principles of management for administration of academic activities are essential for ensuring goal attainment. It is important to treat functions or activities in distance education at par with any industry. Otto Peters (1973)[48] has clearly stated, "distance education system is an academic function, but in industry form in which bulk production of print and media material, and services to students like any service industry are to be met efficiently in a cost-effective manner".

Administrative Division At IGNOU

The administration division[49] of IGNOU provides support to all Divisions, Schools of Studies and statutory authorities and bodies of the University. It performs the following functions:

+ Administration means management of activities connected with keeping records and information processing and applying rules, procedures and policies determined by others. (Dictionary of Management, Dereck French and Heather Saward, (1977) Pan Books Ltd, London, p.9)

(i) Formulation of statues, ordinances, constitution of various bodies, follow up of decisions of various bodies, coordination with MHRD and other educational bodies etc.

(ii) All matters related from recruitment to retirement of non-academic employees of the University, Purchases, Security, Legal Assistance, Housekeeping, Liasoning, and Transport etc.

(iii) SC/ST Cell is also functioning under this division which is the welfare unit for SC and STs.

(iv) In addition, Hindi Cell helps in implementing the official language policy of the government through workshops, programmes and contests to promote Hindi. Translation of official documents is also the responsibility of this Cell.

The administrative sub-system of distance education system as shown in the conceptual model (Figure 2) has been further categorized into three sub-functions. As such, the discussion under this chapter has been presented in the following three sections:

1. Management of Human Resource
2. Management of Financial Resource
3. Management of Library System

MANAGEMENT OF HUMAN RESOURCE AT IGNOU

Organizations exist for people. They are prepared of people and by the people and their effectiveness depends on the behaviour and performance of the people controlling them. The most important asset of any organization is its people.+ The principles and values of the organization are evolved around them. They determine its work culture; their levels of concern and commitment inspire the extent of public confidence in the institution.

+ Human Resource Management deals with management of people in the organization.

(Contd...)

Human resource policy of distance education institutes is a crucial issue. Although education generally is labour intensive enterprise, Distance education can reduce this intensity.

There is generally an established ratio between teacher and students in conventional system. This is primarily, because, there are, for several reasons, constraints on the size of class. A teacher can at best interact only with a certain number of students at a time. Therefore, faculty strength varies with the size of the enrolment. In distance education, situation is very different. Students depend largely on self-instructional material for home-based study. Face-to-face contact is very limited and takes place at different times and at different places.

These flexibilities permit a distance education institute to pursue human resource policies, which are significantly different from those of traditional education. Distance education institute therefore, is an usual mix of personnel—a relatively small core of permanent full time staff consisting of academics, professionals, technocrats and administrative personnel supplemented by a much larger number of part time staff at different locations engaged for specific periods and for specific tasks.

Human Resource Management functions (except staff development and training) at IGNOU is looked after by Administration Division of the university, whereas for staff development and training, the university has set up a full-fledged independent unit known as Staff Training and Research Institute of Distance Education.+

Human resource management is concerned with the people dimension in management. Since every organization is made up of people, acquiring their services, developing their skills motivating them to higher levels of performance and ensuring that they continue to maintain their commitment to the organization are essential to achieving organizational objectives. This is true, regardless of the type of organization –government, business, education, health, recreation or social action. (David.A Decenzo and Stephen. P. Robbins, Personnel/HRM, Third edition, 1989, PHI, New Delhi, p.3)

Manpower Planning+ at IGNOU

Manpower provisions are essential for timely accomplishment of responsibilities and objective achievement.

In simple words, manpower planning as process of forecasting an organization's future demand for, and supply of, the right type of people in the right number. It is only after this, that the human resource management can initiate a recruitment and selection process. Manpower planning facilitates the realization of the organizations objectives by providing the right type and the right number of personnel.

Table 9 depicts the staff position for three categories of Indira Gandhi National Open University for the last five years.

It is well clear from the Table 9 that almost 20% posts are vacant. The respondents from nine divisions have opined that university has no system of manpower planning even after 16 years of its existence. According to respondents only once in the history of university, an exercise, in an ad-hoc manner on the demand of the university employees association was carried out in 1991 and named as Norms Committee Report, which provided some criteria for administrative positions in various Schools/ Divisions/Regional Centres.

Not only this, no manpower planning has been undertaken by the University despite the fact that enrolment in the University has grown from 4500 in 1986 to 3 Lac approximately in 2001. The revenue generation has also increased from 17.5 Lac in 1986 to 105.88 crores approx. in 2001.

+ Manpower planning, recruitment and selection, career advancement, promotion and transfer and performance appraisal functions at IGNOU are reviewed together in this chapter. As the responsibility for staff development and training function at IGNOU has been given separately to Staff Training and Research Institute of Distance Education. The same has been reviewed and apprised separately from the other functions of human resource development.

Table 9
Staff Positions at IGNOU+

Year	*Teachers*			*Academics*			*Administrative*		
	Sanction	*Filled*	*Vacant*	*Sanction*	*Filled*	*Vacant*	*Sanction*	*Filled*	*Vacant*
1997	166	146	20	148	117	31	1260	899	361
1998	199	157	42	148	117	31	1260	875	385
1999	199	146	53	167	136	31	1333	1109	224
2000	199	151	48	167	137	30	1357	1135	222
2001	199	151	48	181	154	27	1357	1114	243

Source: .Based on compilation of data through Annual Reports and other sources.

Further more, the university has been opening Regional Centres year after year, whereas recruitment of personnel to fill the vacant post has not taken place for last four years. Under these circumstances administrative support from the university to Regional Centres is suffering badly. Lack of administrative competence is the cause of all the problems in the university. This hampers delivery of services, monitoring and organization of activities at the Regional Centres. Therefore, it is suggested that university must take immediate steps for filling up vacant posts, in the university and Regional Centres in particular. New Regional Centres should not be created without having proper manpower to carry out the responsibilities at the Regional Centres. This shows the lax situation in the Planning and Development Division, which has not taken steps to plan its manpower requirements. It is high time that Division wakes up and introduces the system of manpower planning on the

+ The staff positions at the university are categorized with the approval of Board of Management, which is its principle decision-making body. Normally, in conventional universities there are two categories of staff i.e., teachers and non-teachers or academics and non-academics but IGNOU has created three categories of staff positions in teachers, academics and non-academics, which is being extended to the personnel in an ad-hoc manner instead through a clearly defined policy.

basis of increased workload in different sub-systems, in different cadres and also establish manpower planning as a process in the system. Otherwise university will not be able to manage its commitment towards students and society.

It is suggested that university should introduce manpower planning, as a regular mechanism to identify the personnel needs taking into consideration following factors:

• Student enrolment	• Number of programmes
• Number of Regional Centres	• Number of learner support centres
• Number of dispatches in a year	• Number of students appearing for Examinations
• Number of assignments evaluated	• Increase in revenue collection
• Number of telecasts and broadcasts	• Number of teleconferencing sessions in a year
• Number of audio video cassettes and CDs produced in a year	• Likely number of programmes to be launched

Manpower planning thus should be an integral component of the planning process of the university otherwise the increase in the student enrolment and programmes will not be sustained and this will finally result in poor quality of student services.

Recruitment and Selection System at IGNOU

After the organization has completed human resource planning process, the next logical step is to hire the right number of people of the right type to fill the jobs. Hiring involves two broad groups of activities: i) Recruitment, and (ii) Selection.

Recruitment is the process of searching for and obtaining applications so as to build a pool of job seekers from whom the right people for the right job can be selected. While selection refers to the process of picking the right candidate from the pool of applications.

It is essential for professional institutions like university to design policies for recruitment and selection of personnel and its strict adherence to avoid favouritism to establish systems process in the university.

Majority of respondents from two Schools, nine Divisions, STRIDE and EMPC feel that university has laid down rules and procedures for recruitment and selection of personnel in the university. Although they feel that these rules and procedures for recruitment and selection of personnel are strictly followed. However, instances of violations of these rules have also been observed. This situation of favouritism is not good for the university as its affects morale of the university employees. Therefore, it is suggested that university should follow rules and regulations uniformally and sincerely for institution building.

Career Advancement and Promotion System at IGNOU

Promotion is transfer of an employee to a new position, which commands higher pay, privileges or status as compared with the old. In other words, it is a vertical movement in rank and responsibility. Career advancement or promotions is the only existing source of motivation in the university system. The staff and officers working in a progressive institution also progress along with the growth of institution. As university has grown multifold, it is essential that staff and officers also progress in the same manner.

Majority of respondents are of the opinion that there are avenues for promotion for the staff of university. There is no doubt that university is growing rapidly. Growth and expansion will result in further creation of posts in different cadres/ systems of the university to sustain the increased workload. The university has the potential to achieve great heights in terms of student enrolment if programmes are launched on the market demand and student services are maintained above par. This will enhance the requirement of staff at various levels resulting in more promotions. As already stated promotions or career advancement means more responsibility and accountability.

This further needs proper training to understand the increased role and responsibilities and perform accordingly. But in the university promotions/career advancement neither means increased responsibility and accountability nor there is any such provision of training. Secondly, the university lacks job specification for different levels and cadres resulting in confusion of roles and responsibilities. Therefore, it is suggested that roles and responsibilities for each post or cadre are clearly defined after undertaking job analysis. This will bring more clarity of roles and responsibilities and increased efficiency in the system.

Transfer policy at IGNOU

Transfer refers to change in which pay, status and privileges of new posts are roughly same as of old. In other words, transfer is a lateral movement of any employee, not involving promotion or demotion. Every organization should have a just, clear-cut and impartial transfer policy, which should be known to each employee.

Majority of respondents feel that there is a transfer policy brought out recently but not implemented in the system sincerely in a transparent manner. The university is a national institution having jurisdiction all over the country. A regional centre is there almost in each State. The university also employs personnel from different parts of the country. Under these circumstances, each staff member would be seeking transfer to his or her native place, which is not feasible. The university has to grow further and further. Therefore, it is suggested that university brings out a transfer policy indicating the basis of transfer, defining the minimum duration at a station etc. delegate authority and ensure its implementation in transparent manner.

Performance appraisal System at IGNOU

Performance appraisal+ is an important tool to evaluate the performance of employees in any system. It is a report on the subordinate by the immediate superior that covers a limited range of aspects like candidate's strengths, weaknesses, major achievements or failures, and information on personality traits and behavioural aspects. This system is widely used for a variety of personnel decisions, particularly transfers and promotions.

Majority of respondents from two Schools, nine Divisions, STRIDE, EMPC and 23 Regional Centres feel that performance appraisal is a continuous process in the university and is also used for promotions of administrative personnel in the university. They also feel that performance appraisal for teachers and academics are not a regular feature however; it is being used for them at the time of career advancement only.

Therefore, it is suggested that performance appraisal system should be sincerely implemented in the university for all categories of personnel at par to keep them alert, motivated and to avoid slackness in their performance. Efforts should also be made to make performance appraisal system more transparent and motivating to improve the performance in the systems of the university.

A review of the forthgoing discussion on human resource management in Indira Gandhi National Open University system reveals that any systematic and regular effort to design and implement effective policies in the area of human resource management has not been made. Therefore, it is suggested that university must have separate human resource division and all the planning with regard to human resource management in this division must be a regular feature. The organization of human resource activities need planning and implementation

---

+ Performance appraisal is the evaluation of an individual's work performance in order to arrive at objective human resource decisions. (Stephen, P. Robbins and Mary Coullter in Management (1998), Prentice Hall of India Pvt. Ltd, New Delhi, p.750)

system and strategy and policies in the area of human resource should be part of system and most important, to have the control system for monitoring the human resource activities.

The human resource policies in distance education institutes especially with reference to Indira Gandhi National Open University should focus on the following:

- Human resource management policies based on trust, openness, equity, consent and consensus;
- built stake and say for people at all levels in categories of staff;
- develop mechanism for identification of personnel needs, assessment procedures and recruitments;
- develop objective performance review and management systems;
- restructure reward systems that are contingent on performance and sustain motivation;
- information sharing, grievances redressal and participation;

MANAGEMENT OF STAFF DEVELOPMENT AND TRAINING AT IGNOU

The personnel policy of any new organization/institute/university must plan for developing the specialized competencies and skills for the personnel deployed in the system. Training process starts from induction of the person in the system. Thereafter, it has to be a regular feature to train the personnel whenever roles and responsibilities change, change in skills and technologies due to advancement of technology.

Training and development is an attempt to improve current and future employee performance by increasing an employee's ability to perform through learning, usually by changing the employee's attitude or increasing his or her skills and knowledge.

Distance education system+ is a new field of education and comparatively a complex one to understand and implement the various components involved and further it has been changing rapidly with developments in the field of computer and information technology. This all demand that training and development aspect of human resource management should be given importance.

Staff Training and Research Institute of Distance Education (STRIDE) looks after the training and development functions in Indira Gandhi National Open University [50].

Functions of STRIDE includes:

- identifying training needs of different categories of personnel, involved in open and distance education;
- building up a resource base of up to date information, training material, resources, expertise and making such resources available whenever needed;
- developing suitable training strategies and relevant material to meet the varied needs of different types of individuals, distance teaching and training institutes;
- organising and coordinating training and staff development activities for the identified target group in institutions through various innovative strategies;
- promoting and involve research in distance and open education at the fundamental, experimental and application levels in order to constantly enrich training programmes, management processes and distance education systems dynamically.

\+ Distance education system is a complex education system and industrial in nature where mass production of print material, audio-video material takes place. Distance education system has all the features of an industry, hence, it becomes imperative that training functions as a systems process on its different aspects like teaching learning methodology, design and development of learning materials in print and media mode, feedback on assignment evaluation and management of examination system like an industrial enterprise.

Identification of training needs in the University

Training should function as a system in the university and identify the training needs of personnel from time to time.

Although the majority of respondents from STRIDE are of the opinion that there are mechanisms for identifying training needs, which is based on the reports of various committees like Administrative Reforms Committee, and performance of staff, change in system. But the opinion of respondents from Divisions, EMPC and Regional Centres is contrary. They believe that STRIDE has failed in meeting its objective of making training a systematic process and to train the personnel in the university. They are of the view that training should be a continuous process in the university so that skills and competencies of staff and officers are sharpened. This will result in increased productivity, efficiency and quality in delivery of student services.

Training material and courses developed by STRIDE

STRIDE is the nodal agency for imparting training to the personnel involved in production of materials, administrative and financial matters, technological areas like computers and media related fields. In addition, it is also responsible for developing learning materials on various subjects related to administrative and financial management in distance education. The training material can be helpful in day-to-day functioning of different sub-system.

Majority of respondents from STRIDE have opined that training material and courses developed by STRIDE during last three years include (1) handbook for development of self learning material, (2) handbook on open and distance education (in press), (3) handbook on assessment and evaluation of distance education (in press), (4) revision of courses of Post Graduate Diploma in Distance Education and Masters of distance education, (5) handbook on counselling and glossary of terms in distance education.

Training materials developed by STRIDE are of academic

nature but no efforts have been made to develop training material on administrative and financial systems and various aspects related to management processes in these areas in the university. The training material produced has also failed to throw light on scheduling of counselling and practical session in the computer programmes having high enrolment, and further how to use various kind of media mix in distance education. Major work done during last three years by STRIDE is still not available for use being in press. STRIDE has good manpower provisions but the division during last three years has done no work to justify the strength as the two programmes launched by STRIDE so far going on since inception of the university.

Opinion of respondents towards training system at IGNOU

Although, the respondents were of the firm opinion that the STRIDE was organizing different training programmes for the staff of university as well as third world countries regularly; however, when enquired respondents from STRIDE failed to provide the details of training programmes organized for third world countries during last three years. The perception and the opinion of respondents from non-STRIDE[+] units were thus contrary.

Respondents from both the Schools have opined that training of teachers in teaching-learning methodology of distance education is a systematic process. Teachers in the university may also be trained in using latest communication and computer technologies to keep pace with the developments, otherwise, it will be difficult for them to cope up when distance education transforms into virtual or electronic mode. Much needs to be done by STRIDE on this front.

All the respondents from Administration and Finance and Accounts Division have categorically stated that STRIDE has not arranged any training programme for them for last many

---

[+] Opinion were obtained from Schools, Divisions, EMPC, Regional Centres and Learner Support Centres

years. The organization of training programmes might have provided relief to both the divisions by improving the efficiency of personnel.

Similarly, all the respondents from Library Division have denied receiving any training from STRIDE. The training programmes should have improved their efficiency and that should have helped them to cope up with the shortage of manpower.

Majority of respondents from EMPC have opined that STRIDE has not organized any training programme for the personnel working at EMPC. STRIDE being a nodal agency for imparting training should have arranged training programmes for improving their skills and competencies in media related activities. This shows that manpower provided to STRIDE is not harnessed fully in the university.

Regional Centres are the field units of the university involved in delivering of student services but majority of respondents have denied receiving any training from STRIDE.

Although 69.09% coordinators of learner support centres stated that they have received training being organised by RSD instead of STRIDE. Unless the coordinators are trained for organization and management of activities of learner support centres they will not understand the importance of various aspects of teaching – learning methodology of distance education system, which is quiet complex. This appears to be main reasons why all the provisioned facilities are not made available to the students at the learner support centres.

54.55% respondents from Regional Centres have stated that majority of academic counsellors doing counselling and providing feedback on assignments to the students are untrained. But they too received training with the coordination of Regional Services Division and Schools. Under these circumstances, the status of counselling, feedback on assignments, audio-video counselling, can be well imagined. Training to all the academic counsellors is essential as it has a direct bearing on student attainment. Therefore, it is suggested that all the untrained academic counsellors and coordinators should be trained adequately to understand the various provisions of distance education system and their role in it.

The conclusion is that the staff development and training has not become a systematic process in the university. Respondents from different sub-systems in majority have stated that training needs of personnel working in the university are not met with. This is affecting the performance of these sub-systems of the university. For example, untrained academic counsellors do counselling, not only this, they are also providing feedback on assignments. This shows that lack of training is affecting the performance of sub-systems in the university and student attainment. The university must ensure that training becomes a systematic process for improving the performance of sub-systems and better student attainment.

Suggestions for improving the staff development and training at IGNOU

Respondents from all the nine Divisions, 22 Regional Centres have strongly opined that training and staff development should be made a systems process and training programmes should be organized regularly for improving the competencies and skills of officers, and staff working in different sub-systems. Training will help in improving the performance and efficiency of the personnel working in the different sub-systems. It will lead of better delivery of student services to the students and increased satisfaction and confidence in the distance education system.

MANAGEMENT OF FINANCIAL RESOURCES AT IGNOU

Traditionally, education has been in the domain of the governments. This was so primarily because education has had no profit motive, and the absence of profits inhibited private initiatives. Education, therefore, depended on public spending, supplemented to a limited extent by religious institutions and public charities. This approach to education changed in the postindustrial society. With the rapid expansion in knowledge and the emergence of science and technology as engines of growth, the need for people with specialized education and training became essential for development. The nature and type of institutions offering education got diversified so did the sources of their funding as well. Even so, the major provider of funds for education in most societies continues to be their governments.[51]

Governments funding meant public spending. And public spending always had strings attached to it. The managers who spent public money were always preoccupied with the concerns of judicious spending, proper accounting and rigorous financial control. In this culture, there was very little scope for modern concepts of financial management like resource mobilization, activity costing and cost control, building up resource bases and taking any risks with finances. In recent times, public spending on education, especially at the higher levels has been progressively declining and therefore it has become necessary to explore alternate channels of funding. In doing so, educational financing is also being progressively influenced by the methods and practices of modern financial management.[52]

Education in India to an extent depends upon government funding, donations etc. The expansion in the field of science and technology as emergence of growth, there is need for specialized education and training for the development of economy and country. There is visible diversification in the nature and type of institutions and in their funding as well. The public funding on education in recent times, especially in the field of higher education has been declining and it has become essential to explore alternate channels of funding. This has also influenced the financial management of government institutions.

The meaningful system of financial control should have following components [53]:

1. periodic reviews of strategic plans to make adjustments in the size and levels of activities to match the expected funding level;

2. reliable systems to forecast the enrolment levels to make realistic assumptions about the fee income;
3. preparation of separate budgets for each cost centre and assessment of the performance of each to determine its productivity and efficiency level;
4. regular and even flow of activities that ensures that the output matches funding and that there are no accumulated shortages of outcomes that might later need additional funding;
5. evaluation of every new proposal for delivery of any service in terms of possible alternative, identifying the benefits relative to the costs;
6. implementation of 'value for money' principles in the systems;
7. finally, by ensuring that all activities contribute towards attainment of objectives;

Role of Finance Committee in Financial Management at IGNOU

Finance Committee of the university is responsible to look after overall financial management+ function of the university. It consists of the Vice-Chancellor as its Chairman, Finance Officer and other members nominated by the Vice-Chancellor including a representative of the Ministry of Human Resources Development.

All the respondents from Finance and Accounts Division are of the opinion that Finance Committee looks after the efficient management/utilization of resources of the university.

\+ Financial management is that managerial activity which is concerned with the planning and controlling of the firms financial resources. (I.M. Pandey, Financial Management, Vikas Publishing House, New Delhi, 1999, p. 3)
It is broadly concerned with the acquisition of funds by a business firm. (Prasanna Chandra, Financial Management, Theory and Practice, Tata-Mcgraw Hill Publishing Co. Ltd, New Delhi, 1999, p. 3)

Finance Committee meetings take place every alternate month normally on the agenda fixed by Finance and Accounts Division. Majority of respondents from Finance and Accounts Division have stated that Finance Committee looks after the management of resources of the university through budget document, annual accounts, and quarterly and half yearly reports. But due to lack of costing mechanism in the Finance and Accounts Division, sometimes it becomes impossible for the Finance Committee to deliberate on the financial management of the university elaborately. Finance Committee should have more members from the field of financial management because teachers as members are hardly able to contribute much towards effective management and supervision of the finances of the university.

Finance and Accounts Division of IGNOU [54] is responsible for following functions:

1. collection of revenue receipt on behalf of University:
2. payment to staff and outside suppliers;
3. preparation and approval of budget estimates from the Finance Committee and Board of Management;
4. review of realization of receipts and expenditure;
5. preparation of annual accounts, investment of the funds of the University;
6. conducting internal audit and liaison with external audit agencies;
7. maintenance of GPF and Welfare fund accounts of the University etc.

The basic objective of financial management should be cost-effectiveness, increased output, and higher rate of return on investment with efficiency in student services.

Collection of revenue and its management at IGNOU

The collection and proper accounting of revenue is essential in any system. Revenue collection in the university is through its Regional Centres is a cumbersome exercise. University as a policy receives fees from students through demand drafts, which is increasing every year with the increase in student enrolment however, but staff strength is more or less same, which is inadequate. It is crucial that revenue collections are properly accounted for in the books of university and reconciled with the admission data.

Table 10

Revenue Collections through Regional Centres during last Five Years

Financial Year	*Revenue Collections (Fees and Sale of Forms) from Regional Centres (in lakhs)*
1996-97	2590.00
1997-98	3200.00
1998-99	4532.00
1999-2000	7570.00
2000-2001	10588.00

Source: Annual Reports, 1996-97 to 2000-2001, IGNOU, New Delhi

All the respondents have opined that revenue receipts of the university are properly accounted for. But it is also a fact that receipt of fees from the students is not properly reconciled. The Finance and Accounts Division remains in dark as to whether all Regional Centres have remitted collections during the same financial year. This is despite clear guidelines to the effect that Regional Centres would not keep more than Rs.1 Lac in their fee account by 7th of any month. Hence neither guidelines are being followed sincerely nor reconciliation mechanism is effective. The delayed transmission of revenue from Regional Centres to Finance and Accounts Division results in loss of interest as Investment Committee in Finance and Accounts Division ensures maximum return on the revenue. There are reports that revenue collection is not timely and reconciliation is ineffective. Therefore, it is suggested that compliance of rules and guidelines should be strictly adhered for efficient financial management of the resources of the University and financial violations should be dealt with a firm hand.

Review of realization of receipts and expenditure

It is essential to monitor the collection of revenue receipts from time to time to ensure that it is accounted properly and expenditure is also related with the income. Hence, it is must to monitor the revenue periodically as it helps in ensuring proper accounting of the same.

Majority of respondents from Finance and Accounts Division have opined that periodicity of review is monthly whereas some respondents have stated the periodicity of review as quarterly and half yearly. Different opinions expressed by the respondents show that officers in Finance and Accounts Division lack knowledge about the periodicity of review of revenue collection and expenditure in the division. It is doubtful whether any such review of realization of receipts and expenditure in the division really takes place. The review of realization of receipts and expenditure should be a regular feature in the Finance and Accounts Division. This will strengthen the financial management of resources in the university. Therefore, authorities should make the review of receipts and expenditure a mandatory process at the division.

Maintenance of fee records of students properly

University receives over 100 crores by way of fees from the students through its Regional Centres. Meticulous financial management requires proper maintenance of fee records of students by the Finance and Accounts Division, which otherwise is also needed for reconciliation purpose.

Majority of respondents from Finance and Accounts Division have opined that fees records of students are properly maintained but one respondent has some apprehension about this and one respondent has categorically stated that it is the responsibility of Regional Services Division. Fee records are also maintained at Student Registration and Evaluation Division in addition to Regional Centres. However, Regional Centres remit fees to Finance and Accounts Division through Regional Services Division. But it is important to mention that overall responsibility of fee collection is of Finance and Accounts Division. Hence, it should devise systems and procedures for proper accounting and reconciliation of fees in the university, for which it is essential that Finance and Accounts Division also maintain fees records of students. The university lacks database management system; otherwise, Finance & Accounts Division can directly reconcile fees received from Regional Centres by using the data from database. In case of discrepancies Regional Centres can be asked reasons for the variation in remittance of fees. Database management will help in simplification of the process. Similarly, Student Registration & Evaluation Division should ensure that student has paid the fees for the programme or course for which result is declared. Fee verification is must before declaration of results in a routine manner. This is essential for any institution to ensure that student pay the fees before declaration of results.

Budget preparation and resource utilization at the University

Budgeting[+] in an institution helps in exercising control over its expenditure. Budget provides a realistic estimate about the planning of the institution that intends to achieve in a given environment. It is also an important standard against which performance can be assessed. Budgeting is a dynamic instrument highlighting the realism, motivation and credibility

---

[+] The term budgeting refers to the managerial process of budget planning and preparation, budgetary control and the related procedures. The final outcome of the budgeting is the preparation of plan, which is popularly designated as a budget. (R.M.Srivastava, Financial Management, Pragati Prakashan, Meerut, 2000,p.230)

A budget is a plan expressed in financial terms; it is a summary of plans financial expenditures and receipts over a period or related to an activity. (Dictionary of Management, Op.cit. P.47)

of the institution. Budgets are also subject to review depending upon the needs of the society and new threats and opportunities in the changed environment.

Expenditure in distance educational institutes can be categorized into two major categories *viz*, Academic, & Administrative expenditure.

Academic expenditure includes teaching-learning activities, research and developmental activities, design and development of print and media materials.

Administrative expenditure includes pay and allowances, personal claims, infrastructure acquisitions and maintenance, campus development, libraries, office automation etc.

Budgeting is of many types *i.e.* zero-based budgeting, performance budgeting, estimated or judgmental budgeting. Presently, emphasis everywhere is on zero-based budgeting.

Table 11

University Budget for last 10 Years

Sl.No.	*Financial Year*	*Revenue Expenditure (in crores)*	*Capital Expenditure (In crores)*
1.	1991-92	15.55	2.59
2.	1992-93	15.16	3.04
3.	1993-94	18.52	3.90
4.	1994-95	20.06	4.86
5.	1995-96	23.94	74.03
6.	1996-97	33.16	9.84
7.	1997-98	43.70	3.17
8.	1998-99	61.29	4.45
9.	1999-2000	102.01	12.38
10.	2000-2001	103.58	10.90

Source: Annual Reports, 1991-92 to 2000-2001, IGNOU.

Majority of respondents from Finance and Accounts Division are of the opinion that estimated or judgmental budgeting is being practiced in the university some of the respondents have expressed diverse opinions, as they are not aware about the kind of budgeting practiced in the university. It is important to mention that Finance and Accounts Division provides direction to all the sub-systems. The opinion of respondents is not a healthy sign for the efficient financial management in the university. To overcome this situation, all officers in the division should be given proper training in all financial matters, as roles and responsibilities are interchangeable in university system.

Majority of respondents from Finance and Accounts Division have opined that resources of the university are utilized as per approved budgetary provisions but in some extreme cases deviations are also made. The response of majority that resources of the university are utilized as per approved budgetary provisions does not appear to be true as there must be occasions when deviation becomes essential due to various reasons. Financial Code of the university provides for re-appropriation to meet exigencies. Reasons given for deviation are following:

- Cost enhancement
- Policy changes and unforeseen circumstances
- Ensure timely release of grants to Regional Centres

Finalization of accounts of the university

Finalization of accounts in time in any institution is indicat[illegible] that financial management is functioning satisfactorily; otherwise, there may be some problems with the financial management of resources in the university.

Majority of respondents from Finance and Accounts Division are of the opinion that university accounts are finalized in time. But internal sources revealed that there have been delays in finalization of accounts and major reason for this is delayed receipt of annual accounts from the Regional Centres. Regional Directors in the university are in semi-academic position and have little knowledge about the financial rules and regulations and University had declared them Drawing and Disbursing Officer. This results in delay in finalization of annual accounts of the Regional Centres. Other reasons for delay in finalization of annual accounts are lack of knowledge among the officers and staff at the Regional Centres and in Finance and Accounts Division. Therefore, it is suggested that all officers and staff of Regional Centres and Finance and Accounts Division should be trained in financial matters to avoid the delay in finalization of annual accounts. This will also result in efficient financial management in the university.

Mechanism for ensuring optimum utilization of resources in the university

The monitoring and control mechanisms designed to check the implementation of plans at every stage of planning helps in optimum utilization of resources and also ensures that efforts remain towards accomplishment of planned objectives, and deviations, if any, are checked in time. Strategies and technology chosen for accomplishment of plans do play a major role in optimum utilization of resources.

Respondents from Planning and Development Division have opined that optimum utilization of resources in the university is through annual and five years plans, periodic trainings and creating awareness on the importance and use of technology. It is surprising that respondents from the Planning and Development Division, who are primarily responsible for cost-efficient planning and optimum utilization of resources, have no clear idea about the optimum utilization of resources of the university. Five year Plans are the long- term plans, basically prepared for sending to the MHRD for obtaining grants etc. The Finance and Accounts Division prepare annual plan by consolidation of annual plans of Schools and Divisions, which are more often arbitrarily decided keeping the past provisions in mind. Therefore, it is suggested, planning should envisage optimum utilization of resources by providing a framework of guidelines for utilization of resources, by choosing best alternative strategy from the available strategies for achieving the targets or planned objectives, quality of the product, input-output ratio, and by putting control/monitoring mechanisms to check the performance and utilization of resources for ensuring cost-effectiveness, and efficiency in the system resulting in optimum utilization of resources. Therefore, it is suggested that strategic planning should be at the core of the university and strategies for implementation should be decided after careful deliberations on the available alternate strategies. Accordingly financial, human and material resources should be provisioned for that purpose. Monitoring or control mechanism must be an inbuilt part of the plans to check the deviations.

Cost-benefit analysis of the schemes before launch

Cost-benefit analysis helps in assessing the cost-effectiveness of available alternatives of achieving a target. Cost-benefit analysis is a critical analysis of given alternatives in terms of cost and features. The university has been providing computer education to its students through government and private institution. Recently, university launched two schemes involving large sums *i.e.,* Regional Computer Laboratories (RCL)/Tele-Learning Centres (TLC) and Special Study Centres (SSC) for the disadvantaged groups of society to reach the un-reached in rural and remote areas.

Respondents from Planning and Development Division have categorically stated that they have no idea about undertaking the cost benefit analysis of the two schemes. The fixed cost of establishing one RCL/TLC is approximately 25 Lac and recurring expenditure towards salaries and maintenance etc. will be in the range of 5-7 Lac p.a. The University has initially established six RC Labs. and eight TLCs. The fixed cost of total project will be in the range of 3.5 to 4.5 crores and recurring expenditure will be around 70-80 Lac p.a., It is surprising that Finance Committee/Board of Management has given clearance to the project of such a magnitude without going into following respects:

- What are the objectives or rationale behind the scheme?

- What will be infrastructure provisions for this purpose?
- What will be the manpower provisions for management of TLCs?
- What cost-benefits will accrue to the University from the project?

Similarly, in the scheme of Special Study Centres a provision has been made for providing furniture and equipment worth 2.5 Lac to each special study centre. The University has not undertaken any pilot or test studies of the scheme and straightway established more than 115 special study centres without seeking approval from the Statutory Bodies like Board of Management through its Student Support Committee and Finance Committee. This again shows that the University has gone ahead with the implementation of the scheme even when it is not approved by various statutory bodies, which is must before making commitment of provisions to the tune of 2.5 crores. Which clearly shows that Planning and Development Division and Finance and Accounts Division have totally failed in their responsibility of evaluation of schemes/projects and financial viability before they are launched formally.

This indicates towards the state of financial management in the university. The University should have defined the objectives of the scheme, infrastructure provisions taking into consideration the requirements at different regional centres under different circumstances; manpower provisions for management of scheme should have been clearly defined and finally the most important, the cost benefit analysis should have been undertaken to have an idea about the expected earnings/ savings from the project to ascertain whether the project is viable one. Therefore, it is suggested that university should considers all these aspects in respect of projects and schemes launched. The functioning of statutory bodies like Finance Committee and Board of Management also needs strengthening so that valuable resources of the University are not drained.

Financial viability for opening regional and learner support centres by IGNOU

University has its Regional offices almost in every state of the country and at some places more than two Regional offices are functioning. Therefore, it becomes imperative to ensure whether financial viability factor is also considered while establishing Regional Centres.

Although majority of respondents from Regional Services Division are of the opinion that financial viability factor is taken into consideration while opening Regional Centres, whereas it is a fact that financial viability factor is not considered while opening Regional Centres. Otherwise, there is no rationale for having two Regional Centres in the State of Jammu and Kashmir. Similarly, Regional Centres of Karnal, Khanna and Shimla are non-viable in terms of student enrolment, expenditure and revenue collections. Establishment of one Regional Centre at Chandigarh will be ideal to meet the needs of three States. As and when number of student increases, number of personnel can also be increased in the same proportion. Presently, Ministry of HRD is cutting the developmental grants for higher education and insisting on generation of internal resources. It becomes more important to minimize the administrative and establishment costs for good financial health of the University.

Similarly, the university has its Learner Support Centres spread throughout the country and at some places more than one Learner Support Centre is functioning even though reasonable student enrolment is not there. The university also invests about Rs.2 Lac on furnishing of each Centre. Therefore, it becomes imperative to consider the financial viability factor while opening Learner Support Centres.

Majority of respondents from Regional Services Division are of the opinion that viability factor is also considered while opening the learner support centres whereas two respondents feels otherwise. The university has about 779 different types of learner support centres and its student enrolment is more than

3 Lac. Distribution of students at the learner support centres is done on the basis of programme, location and type of centre. The students are not evenly distributed at learner support centres. Establishment of learner support centre is not always on merits, sometimes, proposals are also received through various references and pressure groups for opening learner support centres for their own benefits.

The university has the responsibility to cover all the population segments in the country and has to reach the un-reached in rural and remote areas, low female literacy districts, SC/ST, physically handicapped, women and minorities etc. The university has established about 117 special study centres throughout the country and enrolment at these centres is considerably low. It is difficult to consider the financial viability factor while opening learner support centres in these cases. However, efforts should be made to make the centres financially viable as establishment costs on Study Centres and Special Study Centres is about 2 Lac. Expenditure is also incurred towards payment of remuneration of part-time functionaries of these centres, which further adds to the financial liability of the university, particularly, if centres do not have adequate student enrolment. Therefore, all these factors should be borne in mind while opening learner support centres so that valuable resources of the university are saved.

Internal and external audit of accounts and finances of IGNOU

Internal Audit

Internal audit is very useful in building the financial and accounting systems, and checking the wastage and misuse of resources of the university. Internal audit department should ideally function directly under the control of Head of Office and submit its report for his consideration. It helps the Head of Office in having first hand knowledge of the functioning of various departments in the organization or institution.

Majority of respondents from Finance and Accounts Division are of the opinion that internal audit is an integral part of the financial system of the University but one respondent feels otherwise. Internal audit in the University is functioning under Finance and Accounts Division whereas normally it functions under the head of the institution. Internal audit cell in the Finance and Accounts Division is not provided with enough trained manpower to audit the activities of its 23 Regional Centres and about 779 Learner Support Centres. Regional Centres are, therefore, audited on random basis but audit of Learner Support Centres is yet to begin even though the major portion of university budget is spent through them and the part-time functionaries manage them. Therefore, it is suggested that internal audit should be placed directly under the Vice-chancellor and conduct of audit should be made a regular affair for all Regional and Learner Support Centres.

External Audit

The Comptroller and Auditor General of India (CAG) is a statutory authority, which undertakes audit of government offices and organizations. The university is an autonomous body funded by the Ministry of HRD, hence, a provision exists in the IGNOU Act for conduct of audit of accounts of university, by CAG, on annual basis.

Majority of respondents are of the opinion that CAG undertakes accounts and comprehensive audit, whereas, three respondents are of the opinion that only performance audit is undertaken by the CAG. This again substantiates lack of knowledge and awareness about the activities taking place in the Finance and Accounts Division. This indicates that officers in the division lack team spirit and cohesiveness and officers in the division should be assigned responsibilities on rotational basis instead of one officer continuing with the same responsibility for years together.

Serious audit objections raised by CAG

Serious audit objections recently raised by CAG includes:

- Non-recovery of advances within six months

- Non-maintenance of Asset Register
- Non-maintenance of Library Books Stock Register
- Non-submission of utilization certificate by State Open Universities and Correspondence Course Institutes

Objections raised by CAG are very serious in nature, especially one relating to non-submission of utilization certificate by the State Open Universities and Correspondence Course Institutes. Therefore, it is suggested that further grants to defaulters universities/ institutes be stopped and restored only after they submit the utilization certificates in respect of previous grants.

Suggestions for improving the financial management system at IGNOU

Following suggestion are given by the respondents for improving the performance of the division:

- Computerization of accounting systems;
- Providing WAN (Wide Area Network) facility in between Regional Centres and Headquarters of the University;
- Training of personnel in the computerized accounting system;
- Additional staff;
- Fixing of accountability and responsibility, scheduling of activities in the division.

Suggestion given by the respondents from the division for improving the performance is need of the hour. This computerization will help in strengthening the financial management and personnel matters in the university. WAN connectivity will further help in on-line accounting and faster reconciliation and finalization of annual accounts of the university. Computerization will also reduce the demand for more manpower and manpower for conducting audit can be spared from the present personnel strength. The accountability is the essence of success of any system or institution and hence, must be introduced in the system and out performers may be rewarded and incompetent shall be reprimanded. It is must that violations and misuse are dealt strictly.

MANAGEMENT OF LIBRARY SYSTEM AT IGNOU

Distance education is more attuned to learning than teaching, therefore, library has central place in the distance education system. The libraries in distance education operate through three-tier system; viz. central, regional and local. The central library has the characteristics of a general and specialist library. The students in the distance education system must be informed about the provisions available to them at the learner support centres, so that they can avail of these facilities according to their need. Students also need to be informed about the facilities available at the learner support and regional libraries. This on the part of the institution requires that library is supplied with the collection of material and journals that serve as a reference material for their programmes. Staff should also be given proper training for organization and management of libraries and in understanding student needs.

Library and Documentation Division at IGNOU

Library and Documentation Division[55] of IGNOU comprises the Central Library at headquarters as well as Regional Centres and Study Centres. The Central Library caters to the needs of academics, administrative and support staffs while Regional Centre libraries look into the library requirements of the staff of Regional Centre, Learner Support Centre libraries are meant primarily for students, academic counsellors, coordinators locally.

Facilities available at the Central, Regional and Learner Support Centre libraries

Table 12 indicates the type of facilities provided to the staff and students by the Central, Regional and Learner Support Centre libraries of IGNOU.

The Central Library of IGNOU has computerized its housekeeping activities using LibSys package. The complete catalogue of library is now available in computer readable form. This computerized catalogue can be consulted through various access points such as author, title, publisher, series, subject, class number, accession number and any word from the title. One multilingual terminal is available at the library for handling Hindi and other regional language books. The Central Library has microform reader cum printer through which documents in the form of microfilms and microfiches can be consulted.

Table 12

Facilities available at the Central, Regional and Learner Support Centre Libraries

	Central Library	*Regional Library*	*Learner Support Centre Library*
Reading	Yes	Yes	Yes
Lending	Yes	To RC Staff	No
Inter-Library Loan	Yes	No	No
CD - Rom Based Service	Yes	No	No
Internet Based Service	Yes	No	No
Del-net Based Service	Yes	No	No

Source: Respondents from Library and Documentation Division

The services offered by the Central Library: Reading, Lending, Reference, Referral, Inter Library Loan, Documentation, Bibliographies, Online Public Access Catalogue, CD-Rom based services, Microform Search facility, Internet and Delnet based services, Reprographic, Lamination, Spiral binding and CD-Networking Services.

From the Table 12 it is clear that the libraries at the Regional and Learner Support Centre are not serving any useful purpose to the students. The students are not allowed lending facility either from the Regional or Learner Support Centre libraries. Therefore, university may either consider for strengthening the library facilities after taking feedback studies for their optimum utilization or alternative strategies of providing library facilities to the students may be explored.

The university is in the process of providing computers with internet facility to the learner support centres and students may be provided the facilities of E-Libraries or any other viable strategy may be considered on the expertise of librarian in the university or feedback studies on utilization of libraries may be undertaken. The guidelines of Distance Education Council should be followed as suggested by respondents from the Library and Documentation Division.

Mechanism for procurement of books and journals at Central, Regional and learner Support Centre Libraries

Central library of IGNOU procures books and journals for the Central, Regional and Learner Support Centre libraries. There should be a policy of university on the kind of books to be supplied to Regional and Learner Support Centre libraries. Regional Centres have been delegated powers to purchase journals as per laid down guidelines.

All the respondents are of the opinion that prescribed acquisition policy of the university for procurement of books and journals in the central library is being followed strictly. It is in order to have a written policy for acquisition of books and journals for such a large system. It helps in proper organization and convenient utilization of library facilities. Further, it is more important to implement the laid down policy systematically in the university. But respondents from Finance and Accounts Division have opined that CAG has indicted the University for its failure to maintain accession registers for the holding. Therefore, it is suggested that computerized inventory of library holding including that of Regional and Learner Support Centres of the University be maintained to avoid such strictures from statutory agencies.

There is also a provision of library at all the Regional Centres of the University. Majority of respondents have opined that procurement of journals are delegated to the Regional

Centres for the libraries at the Regional Centres however, books are procured by the central library and sent to the Regional Centres. Regional Centres are delegated powers to procure books and journal within certain financial limit, which is insufficient for proper organization of library facilities. However, no laid down policies or guidelines for procurement of books and journals for Regional Centres exists. The arbitrary powers always lead to misuse of power. Therefore, it is suggested that a written policy be designed and powers be delegated to the Regional Centres for its implementation. Libraries at the Regional Centres need to be strengthened by delegating more financial powers so that students enrolled with the Regional Centre can avail library facilities. However, university may while devising a policy for the Regional Centres, collect the data of students availing the library facilities at the Regional Centres. Regional Centres of the University have enrolment more than that of State Open Universities. Libraries of the Regional Centres, therefore, need to be developed as full-fledged libraries to meet the demand of students, academic counsellors, staff members etc.

Books are also supplied to the Learner Support Centres from the Central Library and there is no provision of supplying journals to Learner Support Centres at present.

Majority of respondents from library and documentation division have opined that there is no defined policy for procurement of books and journals at the learner support centres. Learner Support Centres are not delegated powers for procurement of books and journals. According to the concept and provisions of distance education, libraries at the learner support centres are to be maintained for supplementing the study material supplied by the university. The part-time functionaries of the host institution manage learner support centres and it is difficult for them to make good library facilities available to the students attached to the centre. Students in their responses have pointed out that library facilities provided by the university are not properly organized and are inadequate. The University should strengthen libraries at the learner support centres after undertaking feedback studies on utilization of library facilities. The basic issues involved in proper organization and management of library at the leaner support centres are, provision of space, trained manpower and optimum utilization of libraries. Keeping all these aspects in view, alternate strategies for meeting the library needs of students, in cost-effective manner like introduction of e-library or utilization of the libraries of the host institution needs to be explored. The university may consider of making use of libraries of host institute, a mandatory condition for opening learner support centre. This will help the university in saving its valuable resources.

Suggestions for improving the performance of libraries at IGNOU

In order to improve the access of library to the student community by proper planning, management, coordination between central, regional and learner centre libraries is essential. For proper utilization, libraries should be opened on weekends. The process of decentralization should be expedited to Regional Centres. For improving the performance of library division, the division should be provided adequate staff, space and infrastructure facilities to become digital/electronic library.

Chapter 6

MANAGEMENT OF ACADEMIC SYSTEM AT IGNOU

The heart of any distance education system is its academic offerings and media support system for transmitting those academic programmes to the distant students. Thus, academic system of any open university can be categorized into two sub-systems, as follows:

1.Management of Academic Programmes

2.Management of Media Support System

In the following section of this chapter, an attempt has been made by the researcher to appraise these two different but inter-related aspects of academic system of Indira Gandhi National Open University.

Management of Academic Programmes at IGNOU

The major concerns of the university's programmes are its academic offerings. Academic programmes are developed to fulfill the thirst of knowledge of a population segment. The basic objective of acquiring knowledge is to settle in life by acquiring professional and other kind of certification to get a job for his or her lifetime. Some programmes are creativity oriented; those help them in their day-to-day use. These have to be designed and developed by the Schools of Studies. The Planning and Development Division of the university works in cooperation with the Schools in providing them with relevant information and assisting them in developing their proposal as specific projects for consideration at various levels. Number of programmes being offered by 9 Schools of the university is shown in Exhibit I.

The basis of launching a new academic programme by the university

The basis of launching a programme is market demand, need survey, viability. Among these, viability of programme is a very significant factor to keep in mind. Reports of manpower planning by Institute of Applied Manpower Research, data from Census of India and reports and studies of similar organizations can form the basis for launching a programme.

All the respondents from both the Schools have indicated following basis for launching a new academic programme by the university:

- Market demand and need of the programme
- Demand factors and standardized programmes
- Need survey, target audience, viability and social relevance
- Usefulness for development of human skills
- Collaborative programmes
- Up-gradation of old course

The basis for launching programmes are the one defined or outlined in the project report for the establishment of University. The most successful programmes launched by the university attracting large student enrolment are from the Schools of Computer and Management having 50% and 15% enrolment respectively. The remaining 55 programmes comprise 35% of enrolment indicating that all these lack in market demand and usefulness in development of human skills except B.Ed, Nursing etc. that has limited seats fixed by respective controlling bodies like National Council for Teacher Education and Nursing Council of India.

Process of acceptance of a programme for development

The process of acceptance of a programme for development should be on the basis of various reports regarding manpower requirements in the country so that resources invested on design and development of a programme are utilized for development of human skills and competencies aimed at development and growth of society and country. Researches can be of valuable help in this regard.

Respondents from the Schools have stated following mechanism for acceptance of the programme for development:

- The proposal is submitted to School Board, Academic Council considering suitability in terms of need, viability, social relevance etc.
- Programme for development is accepted on the recommendations of School Board, Planning Board and Academic Council.
- The idea from experts in the field for meeting the need of society.
- The discussion groups identify the programme; the proposal is submitted through School Board, which is followed by Academic Councils approval.
- The process is standardized across the Schools.
- On the positive response from need survey, target audience and collaborations with target groups etc.
- The programme should provide a strong theoretical background with a strong view of latest technological trends of the market.
- On the basis of pilot study.

The process for programme acceptance is standardized for all the Schools in the university but the low student enrolment in about 40 programmes indicate that programmes lack demand among the people and indicate towards deficiencies in need survey, target audience if at all conducted. Even the, Academic

Council of the University has approved these programmes for launch without going into the depth. The programme acceptance should be based on the need, viability and market acceptance of the programme. The university at present offers about 65 programmes but management and computer programmes of the university has major share of student enrolment *i.e.* about 65% of the total enrolment of the university. This indicates that remaining programmes launched by the university are non-viable in majority and lack demand among students. This shows that feedback studies before undertaking development and launch of programme are not carried out. It also puts a question mark on the procedure of acceptance of the programme for launch, as it has proved ineffective. This results in wastage of national resources. Hence, market research or need is an important factor to be taken into consideration while accepting the programme for development.

Factors taken into consideration while designing programme curriculum

Programme curriculum is the most important factor while designing the programme. Curriculum should be at par with international standards and there should be in-built Total Quality Management (TQM) provisions. Evaluation methodology should also be kept at par with international standards so that the produce is able to withstand all kind of testing in the job market.

The respondents from Schools have indicated that following factors are taken into consideration while designing the programme curriculum:

- Recent developments in that field or course or programme, difficulty level, learning hours and target group.
- Latest trends and changes.
- Curriculum should be at par with other universities launching similar programmes, new courses be added according to the need of the hour and availability of infrastructure.

- Industry requirements, student needs and availability of resources.
- As suggested by Expert Committee, which includes eminent academics, user organizations, bases are similar for curriculum of other organizations and specific needs of the programme.
- Language, usefulness, standards of the programme to the society at large.
- On the basis of inputs considered necessary for knowledge and skills for the career.
- To be suitable to the target groups.
- Strong theory background, Development time for the programme, resource availability in general etc.
- Inputs from experts of the industry, syllabus in qualifying examinations and level of programme.

The factors taken into consideration while designing the programme curriculum are recent developments in that field of course or programme, difficulty level, learning hours and target group. In addition to this, industry requirements, student needs and availability of resources are other considerations. Programme curriculum is further discussed in the Expert Committee, which includes eminent academics, user organizations; basis are similar for curriculum of other organizations and specific needs of the programme. This shows that factors for designing the programmes are not standardized across the Schools of University. It appears that faculty members are not clear about the factors taken into consideration for designing the programme curriculum. Most important factor is deciding the programme curriculum that it should be at par with international standard and latest innovation in the field are incorporated so that the produce is able to compete in the job market in terms of knowledge and skills. Shortage of resources should not be a constraining factor.

Inputs for planning the Academic Calendar of the University

Academic planning of the university is about the programmes to be launched, programme curriculum and strategies for their launch etc. Academic planning should take inputs from Schools regarding programmes considered for launch and their objectives, their curriculum, strategy for their launch, student enrolment, likely revenue generation from the programme. Other factors include fees structure, development of study material, requirement of personnel, training needs etc.

Respondents from Planning and Development Division have indicated that factors that go in the academic planning of the university are inputs from academic programme committee and F & A Division. This shows that respondents in Planning Division have no clear idea about the planning process in the university. Inputs that go into the planning of the academic calendar of the university includes:

- Inputs from Schools about the launch of new academic programmes;
- Inputs from Regional Service Division on expansion of network of learner support services i.e. establishment of Regional and Leaner Support Centres;
- Inputs from STRIDE on the training programmes;
- Inputs from Finance and Accounts Division on resource planning;
- Inputs from Students Registration and Evaluation Division on conduct of examinations and assignment evaluation;
- Inputs from Administration and Academic Coordination Division on the likely manpower requirements and research needs, and so on.

All these inputs constitute annual plan of the university for which financial provisions are derived from the financial estimates of Schools and Divisions and provisions are made after its careful examination and considering the availability of resources in the university but in practice, manpower provisions at different levels are not ensured, resulting work pressure on existing personnel for management and organization of various services for the programme.

Mechanism for ensuring quality of produce in different modes

The programmes launched by the university should have quality maintenance measures in different modes like print, media, counselling, teleconferencing etc. Distance education system has to supplement the lack of face-to-face interface through different modes of teaching; hence all qualitative measures need special attention.

It is clear that respondents from Schools differ in their responses on the mechanism for ensuring quality of produce in different modes whereas, there should have been well defined and articulated policy for ensuring the quality of produce in different modes like print, audio, video, teleconferencing, and counselling etc. However, the opinion of all the respondents put together provides a detailed outline for policy framework for ensuring the quality of produce in different modes. This difference of opinion indicates that either university lacks a well defined policy for maintaining quality under different medias or faculty members are not aware about the policy of the university in this regard.

Student's perception towards quality of study material

All the students were asked to appraise the quality of study material supplied to them. Their opinions and perceptions towards different aspects of quality of the study material have been presented in Table 13 below.

Table 13

Student's perception on different aspects of study material

Features of quality of study material	*No. of Respondents*						
	Yes		*No*		*No response*		*Total response*
The overall standard of study material is high	220	(71.66)	72	(23.45)	15	(4.89)	307
The quality of study material is uniform throughout the course	225	(73.29)	56	(18.24)	26	(8.47)	307
Chapters and contents are arranged in logical manner	253	(82.21)	36	(12.08)	18	(5.71)	307
The contents are clear and easy to comprehend	211	(68.73)	82	(26.71)	14	(4.56)	307
The study material is precise and to the point	216	(70.36)	72	(23.45)	19	(6.91)	307
An adequate coverage was given to all topics of the course	178	(57.98)	112	(36.48)	17	(5.54)	307
There was need for additional reference material	218	(71.01)	69	(22.48)	20	(6.51)	307
Student exercise and self assessment tests are adequate	191	(62.21)	87	(28.34)	29	(9.45)	307
Student exercise and self assessment tests are useful	189	(61.56)	54	(17.59)	64	(20.85)	307

Source: Responses received from Students.

As shown in Table 13 above, 71.66% students have found the quality of study material of very high order and 23.45% students do not find the quality of study material good enough and 4.89% have remained silent. The university has maintained the quality of its material and has also received the 'Centre of Excellence' award from Commonwealth of Learning,

Vancouver, but timely delivery to students needs to be ensured, so that they make good use of its quality. Secondly, quality of study material will only be useful if properly supplemented with other kinds of media like audio-video, teleconferencing etc. Other aspects of student delivery also need to be strengthened so that students can avail full advantage of the provisions made for them in the distance education system.

Further 73.29% student fraternity feels that quality of study material supplied to them is uniform in all the courses of study, 18.24% students do not feel so and 8.47% are silent. The courses of a programme are designed and developed with the help and cooperation of faculty members and experts identified in that field from various institutes throughout the country. There can be marginal difference here and there but overall quality maintenance measures are ensured in the university and that is the reason students have not found much difference in quality of courses. The university should continue to maintain the quality of study material for all its programmes launched in future also.

In opinion of 82.21% students, chapters and contents in the study material are arranged in logical manner and only 12.08% students do not find the presentation of chapters and contents in the study material logical and 5.71% students are silent. Here also student fraternity feels more than satisfied. This shows that process related to design and development of study material is working efficiently and distance education system is a very good and sustainable system of study.

Two third of students feel contents in the study material are clear and easy to comprehend and 26.71% students have some difficulty in comprehension and 4.56% students are silent. This aspect of design and development of study material needs consideration at Schools for making efforts to use simple language so that contents are easy to comprehend by the students. The faculty members and course writers should use more simple vocabulary of the language in which material is designed. Similarly, translators can also be advised to translate the material using simple vocabulary of the language while translating the study material in regional language.

The study material is found to be precise and to the point according to 70.36% of students, while 23.45% students do not find the study material precise and to the point and 6.19% students are silent. The University is adopting all measures for maintaining the quality of study material. However 23.45% students who have opined otherwise should always be kept in mind for bringing further improvement in the quality of study material so that student attainment is higher. Therefore, it should be ensured that inputs in the study material are presented precisely in simple language and to the point.

In Table 13, 57.98% students have indicated that adequate coverage is given to all topics of the course in the study material, whereas, 36.48% students do not feel so and 5.54% are silent. Even though majority of students feel that adequate coverage to all topics of the course are given in the study material, responses of 36.48% students needs consideration. Wider coverage to all the topics in programme curriculum should be ensured, especially in case of computer programmes that all latest innovations and developments are included in the course curriculum. This necessitates early revision of course material of computer programmes as changes in the field of computer technology are taking place at much faster pace. Therefore, university may adopt more professional approach by considering latest topics while designing course curriculum especially in case of computer and management courses.

71.01% students in Table 13 feel the need for additional reference material but 22.48% are of the opinion that there is no need of additional reference material in addition to study material provided by the university and 6.51% students are silent. The planning and designing of course or programme curriculum needs a rethinking in view of responses from majority of students. Changes in the field of computer technology and management education are taking place at a faster pace. This may be the reason that, student, feel the need for additional reference material. Still, teachers in the field of computer and management in the University should consider the opinion expressed by the students for an early review of courseware.

As per Table 13 students majority (62.21%) find self-exercises and self-assessment test given in the course material adequate but 28.34% students feel the need for incorporating more student exercises and self-assessment tests in the study material and 9.45% students are silent. The responses of students need attention of experts involved in course/ curriculum design in distance education mode, how best the need of the students for more students-exercises and self-assessment tests can be met with. The possibility of using teleconferencing, telecast and internet facilities especially in case of students of computer programmes for self-exercises and self -assessment tests may be explored.

Table 13 shows that 61.56% students have found student exercises and self -assessment tests useful, however, 17.59% students do not find student exercises and self-assessment tests useful and 20.85% are silent. The opinion of majority of students is an indication that student exercises and self- assessment tests are playing a useful and vital role in their accomplishment but continuous efforts by the university are needed for maintaining the creativity and interest of students in these exercises for better enrichment in distance education system.

Selection of various types of media mix for teaching-learning methodology

Distance education system uses multi-media approach in its teaching-learning methodology. The basic question that needs to be addressed is how to decide on the judicious mix of various kinds of media like print, audio, video, teleconferencing, telecast and broadcast.

Respondents from Schools on the issue of basis for selection of various types of media mix indicates that faculty members are not aware about the policy of the university for selection of various kinds of media and its extent. It is the basic responsibility of faculty members to understand the teaching-learning methodology and role of each media for making a judicious mix in distance education system. The faculty members are also given one increment for completion of postgraduate diploma in distance education and rationale is to bring clarity among the faculty members in determining the basis for selection for various kinds of media and their importance in distance education teaching learning methodology. The response indicates towards an adequate training to the teachers to understand the role of multi-media in distance education.

Inbuilt parts of the academic programme

According to the respondents from the Schools, evaluation methodology, feedback and certification are an in-built part of the programme. It is essential for any programme of study that it defines evaluation mechanism, feedback mechanism and the level of certification on completion of the programme. It help students in understanding the level of programme, kind of feedback and evaluation strategy adopted during study and finally its usefulness for them.

Mechanism to bring quality in learner achievement

Students of distance education system lack face-to-face interface like that available in conventional education system. It is said that in distance education, mechanism for brining quality in learner achievement are in-built.

Majority of respondents from the Schools have detailed following mechanism for bringing quality in learner achievement:

- Through self-instructional materials, curriculum design and appropriate audio-video inputs.
- By using multi-media approach.
- Through high quality of assignments, term-end exams, and teleconferencing.
- Term-end exams, self test exercises and through projects.

- Advance planning, commitment of persons involved.
- Strict evaluation system
- Through feedback on evaluated assignments.
- High quality of materials, timely delivery of materials.

All the responses combining together, makes a mechanism for bringing in quality of learner achievement. The first step in learner achievement is to provide self-learning material designed on the basis of structural system of distance education methodology added with audio-video, teleconferencing, telecast and broadcast. This is further added with strong feedback and evaluation system through assignments and term-end examinations. The provisions for learner achievement through programme are excellent. But it is more important that these facilities are also utilised properly so that students get the real benefit from the programmes of studies in the distance education system. Therefore, efforts are needed to provide all the provisioned facilities in time and systematic manner to ensure better learner attainment.

Suggestions for improving the performance of Schools

Respondents from Schools have suggested for more participation in seminars, conferences and training etc., flexibility in managing course schedule and participation of faculty members in decision making. In addition, it is suggested that the system of accountability, participation in monitoring of programme activities at the field level needs to be introduced. The researches on programme evaluation; system evaluation should form part of duties and responsibilities of Schools, aimed at improving the quality of student services.

MANAGEMENT OF MEDIA SUPPORT SYSTEM AT IGNOU

The distance education system before advent of electronic media was considered a passive mode of instruction lacking in interest and enthusiasm.

Modern science and technology has placed variety of electronic based instructional aids at the disposal of the educators and learners that plays a significant role for a developing country like ours in reaching the unreached. Communication media and technology has changed the total scenario in distance education system by improving the quality of instruction. The newer technologies like audio-video, CDs, television, radio and teleconferencing etc., have provided an added advantage to the distance education in reaching the unreached population segment. The technology has helped in reducing the distances between institutes and the learner. Another, important advantage of technology is that it helps in maintaining the standards of quality in distance education material in media components, as a powerful medium of delivery. Technology component may be costlier initially but on an average it is cheaper than conventional education system.

The crucial factor is to determine the judicious media mix in distance education system and networking of distance education institutes, which will further prove cost-effective. The major research studies exclusively on identifying the judicious media mix are the need of the time as technology obsoletion is very fast. Therefore, the identified judicious mix should be carefully chosen keeping the ongoing developments in the field of technology to reap its benefits.

The country possesses a good network of satellite and almost all the parts of the country are within the reach of radio and television network. The Government of India has also launched an Education Channel 'Gyan Darshan' recently in consortium mode involving national and international agencies. Similarly, university is in the process of launching 'Gyan Vani' very shortly. The university also possesses a good infrastructure of communication facilities and what needs to be ensured is its fullest utilization in delivery of student services. This will help in maintenance of quality in cost-effective and efficient manner.

Electronic Media Production Centre[56] was established under a technical collaboration programme with the Japan International Cooperation Agency of the Government of Japan.

This is primarily involved in the production of audio-video courseware for the academic programmes of the IGNOU. It is equipped with the state of the art media facilities: two large video studios, two digital audio studios, Betacem SP edit suites, audio editing suites, a large cassette duplication plant, computer animation system etc. These facilities are available for use by other educational institutions and State open Universities. In addition, training, academic and research activities in media related areas are also undertaken.

Educational Channel 'Gyan Darshan' at IGNOU

The national network of Doordarshan telecast the video programmes produced by this centre on all days of the week. Similarly the audio programmes are broadcast through select stations of AIR. Recently, a 15 minutes educational news magazine programme "Darpan" is also being produced for telecast through Doordarshan's News channel daily and with the provision of repeat telecast on the same day. The Ministry of Human Resources Development has also entrusted the responsibility of educational channel 'Gyan Darshan' to Indira Gandhi National Open University, which is being managed by EMPC.

Majority of respondents from Electronic Media Production Centre are of the opinion that 'Gyan Darshan', an educational channel launched by the University is meeting its objectives though some respondents do not seem to agree. It is too early to comment on the performance or achievement of objectives by 'Gyan Darshan', but it is a fact, that the programmes of Gyan Darshan are not available in many States. Arrangements are being made to ensure transmission of its programmes throughout the country. The university should have made all the arrangements for transmission of its programmes before launch. Otherwise, due to non-availability of transmission of programmes to the students and other users national resources are going waste. Lately, university is tying up with cable operators for telecast of its programmes throughout the country but barring two or three States. The programmes are not yet available for the viewers.

Audio-Video

In addition to the broadcast mode, the educational audios and videos are duplicated on to audio cassettes and VHS cassettes for distribution to Regional and Study Centres for use as part of audio-video counselling. These cassettes are also available for sale at nominal prices. The audio-video facility provided by EMPC through learner support centres, have however been rated as poor, by the students.

Teleconferencing

Regular interactive teleconferencing+ sessions are conducted through the Training and Development Communication Channel (TDCC), which is a one-way video and two-way audio satellite based teleconferencing facility on extended C-band jointly managed by ISRO and University. Presently it links IGNOU with approximately 175 receiving nodes of which 22 are located at Regional Centres, 6 at State Open Universities and over 150 Learner Support Centres of the University. Very recently, teleconferencing has been further extended to 148 more Learner Support Centres under its Women Empowerment Programme. But the number of Learner Support Centres has increased to 779, which shows that EMPC has failed in providing teleconferencing dish to more than 50% Learner Support Centres. Therefore, it is suggested all the remaining Learner Support Centres should be provided with teleconferencing facility immediately. It should be further ensured by EMPC that all the new Learner Support Centres are provided teleconferencing facility as and when they are established.

+ Teleconferencing is a system, which helps in transmitting the one-way video and two-way audio interface in between student and the teacher at different nodes throughout the country. The university has installed about 320 such nodes throughout the country. It makes possible uniform quality of counselling a reality. For quiet some, university used as a tool for transmitting 40% counselling in management programme. Similarly, it can be used for induction programmes, training programmes for academic counsellors and coordinators etc.

Teleconferencing is a very potent medium for imparting counselling, induction programmes and orientation of coordinators and academic counsellors resulting improvement in quality of student services. It will result in huge savings to the university and also help in maintaining the quality of its media services offered to the students centrally and also ensure optimum utilization of its media facilities created by the university.

Students were asked to rate the audio, video and teleconferencing facilities provided to them by IGNOU. Opinions received are shown in Table 14 below.

Table 14

Opinion of students towards Audio, Video and Teleconferencing facilities

Facility		*Rating*		*Weighted Average*
Weight	Good 3	Average 2	Poor 1	
Audio	19	75	213	1.1
Video	12	25	270	1.1
Teleconferencing	10	38	260	1.1

Source: Based on the responses of student.

The weighted average of 1.1 students responses in Table 14 towards audio facilities provided by the university indicates that audio facilities as envisaged in distance education system have completely failed to provide desired input to the students. The university should look into all the stages of delivery of audio facilities and organization of audio sessions for the students at the Learner Support Centres. This indicates that either EMPC has failed in producing and making audio programmes available to the Learner Support Centres or Learner Support Centres have failed to organize audio sessions for the students. This aspect of organization of audio sessions at the Learner Support Centres also requires closer monitoring.

Similarly, video services of the university have also failed in achieving its objective of facilitating the students and are rated by students as poor. As suggested in case of audio facilities, video facilities also need closer monitoring so that video sessions are organized for the students at the Learner Support Centres. The university should strengthen its monitoring systems so that situation is not worsened further and students are benefited in accordance with the concept of distance education system and its teaching-learning methodology.

Teleconferencing is also completely ineffective. Teleconferencing is a good facility that can help university in providing good quality of counselling for their programmes in cost-effective manner. Students in their responses have also pointed out that teleconferencing is not held as per schedule and learner support centres have not informed them about the teleconferencing schedule well in advance. Teleconferencing has the potential of cutting geographical barriers and reaching the un-reached, which is the sole objective and benefit of studying in distance education.

Electronic Media Production Centre is built with an aid of about Rs. 70 crore and during its functioning of more than 5 years. It has failed to deliver goods to the students. The media component is the distinguishing factor in the distance education teaching-learning methodology, which provides it an advantage over correspondence education. If the state of the affairs in a national Open University is like this, which is responsible for maintaining the standards of quality in distance education system, the situation of other Distance Teaching Institutes and State Open Universities can be well imagined. The opinion above shows that university has completely failed in providing multi-media teaching as claimed by it. The pathetic situation of providing media services clearly states that university has no proper planning, organization, monitoring mechanism and control system for ensuring that all the provisioned media services are delivered to the students in time effectively. In view of the situation presented by the students in their responses, it is suggested that delivery of audio-video material be decentralized to the Regional Centres as it would be easier for them to deliver and monitor the utilization of media related services at the learner support centres in their region. From the above, it emerges that either university has no monitoring and control mechanism existing system is totally ineffective in improving the media services in the university. Further, it is added that EMPC is an autonomous organization, which has complete administrative and financial autonomy for its functioning. The purpose of granting functional autonomy to the EMPC has also failed in its objectives as the students are deprived of their rightful services, which is criminal on the part of university. Regional Services Division through its Regional Centres monitors the activities of Regional and learner support centres and also coordinates with the EMPC for organization of media facilities. Despite this, Regional Services Division has also completely failed in pointing out towards failure in conduct of audio-video and teleconferencing services to the student during last 5 years. On the other hand, university has supplied colour televisions, audio systems, and VCDs etc, worth more than three crore to its Regional and Learner Support Centres, throughout the country. The equipment is also lying unutilized. This is clearly wastage of national resources provided to the university for promoting distance education system in the country. Finally, university should take this system failure on part of EMPC seriously and all non-performing should be dealt with a firm hand. Immediate steps to streamline different aspects of audio-video and teleconferencing operations needs to be initiated for the real benefit of multi-media approach to the students in distance education system.

Conducting feasibility studies before launch of telecast and broadcast facilities

Majority of respondents from EMPC and schools are of the opinion that feasibility studies are not conducted before launch of telecast and broadcast of IGNOU programmes. This indicates that activities are launched without undertaking feedback studies, market survey and need assessment. The launch of various kinds of media activities involves huge sums. It is surprising that decisions involving such large amount are taken without feedback about the success and viability of these activities. It would have been better if relevant statistics are collected and analyzed before taking decisions. It would have been better if university had undertaken the radio counselling initially as this facility is available throughout the country. This speaks about the kind of planning and management systems that are prevalent in the university.

Suggestions for improving the performance of media support system

Respondents from Electronic Media Production Centre have suggested that planning should start from root to higher level and favouritism from top management be totally stopped. Gyan Darshan and Gyan Vani should be in project mode and should not form part of EMPC. More administrative staff to handle the increased workload should be provided and performance based incentives, inclusion of professionals in advisory and policy planning should be ensured.

Suggestion of respondents from EMPC points out for proper planning in its activities and to stop prevalent favouritism. Professionalism and team spirit needs to be strengthened for meeting its laid down objectives and to compete with private sector. To attain professionalism there should be provision of performance based incentives and professional should be included in policy planning mechanism of EMPC and adhocism should be avoided to bring systems process. In addition to above, organization of activities at EMPC also need closer monitoring at all levels.

Chapter 7

MANAGEMENT OF RESEARCH FUNCTION AT IGNOU

Research plays an important role in effective management of distance education system. The main management functions are planning, organizing, implementing, and controlling. The efficacy of all these functions is dependent on the inputs in the form of information, which assist, in decision-making, organizing and effective implementation of the decision. The research helps to provide such information. The research in distance education can be categorized in two major areas:

- System Evaluation, and
- Programme Evaluation.

The research in distance education can be designed and taken up at the system level and at programme level. System evaluation research includes basic measures of functions like collection and compilation of basic information like student enrolment, number of programmes, revenue generation and unit cost etc, efficiency standards like input-out put ratio, rate of drop outs, average time for completion of programme etc. Objective achievement in terms of access, opportunities, equity and some specific needs analysis of student composition. Policy and practices *i.e.* market survey, need assessment, market acceptability of the output, costing from systems and students point of view, diversification or extension activities and institutional like organizational structure, conceptual model, personnel policies, financial management etc.[57]

Similarly, programme evaluation research could include formative evaluation and summative evaluation. Formative evaluation of materials by trying them on the past students to obtain feedback and also seeking comments from internal and external experts before finalization. Summative evaluation like getting feedback from the students, evaluation of teaching–learning strategies vis-à-vis outcome, presentation styles, currency of content etc.[58]

RESEARCH SYSTEM AT IGNOU

Academic Coordination Division[59] of the University is responsible for research and development in the field of distance education. The research policy of the university is to promote subject based and discipline based areas, developmental studies, interdisciplinary studies and system based areas. Distance education system is a new field of education and has enough potential for research on various aspects of system development and programme evaluation. However, action research is always preferred. To implement the research strategy at IGNOU, following specific research plans have been envisaged:

- Research projects scheme for the University staff and academics from other institutions all over the country;
- Research degree programmes leading to the award of M.Phil/Ph.D;
- Research fellowship and associateships, and
- Publication of research studies.

The University has already implemented the research project scheme, under which there are two types of research projects, one attracting funding up to Rs.30, 000 and other up to Rs. 2,00,000. The University has already launched Ph.D. programmes in Education. The research fellowship scheme has been integrated with the M.Phil / Ph.D programmes of the University. Research Council has been constituted to manage and coordinate all the research activities of the University.

Respondents from Academic Coordination Division have opined that the research studies are undertaken from time to time in the university. But the impact of research studies undertaken for improving the systems, programmes development; institution building and organization development is not visible. This indicates either the researches are not focused or lacks in quality and therefore, not considered good enough for system improvement. Indira Gandhi National Open University is a national/ international university and also an apex body for promoting equity and excellence in the country in the field of distance education. Therefore, it is suggested that university should promote research on different sub-systems of distance education by providing themes for the action research so that systems in the university are strengthened for attaining its objectives in a qualitative manner.

Objectives of research function at IGNOU

Respondents have opined that the main objective of the researches undertaken in the university is for improvement in system and quality of programme and finally in delivery of its services, which are of complex nature. But objective remains unfulfilled, as these researches are not considered or made use of while designing sub-systems of distance education. Similarly, policy-planning mechanism is not based on the outcome of the researches undertaken, and unless this is done, the policy planning will remain futile exercise; in the long run the absence of development strategies may even jeopardize the success of concept of distance education in the country.

Thrust areas of research at IGNOU

Thrust areas of the research and development for the university should be system development and evaluation of ongoing programmes, delivery of student services and convergence of educational systems. The research should result in improvement of its student support services by development of training kits for beginners in distance education system.

Although the university undertakes lot of research activities regularly, improvement in the systems/ sub-systems and quality of programme delivery is not visible. It shows that the research programmes undertaken are not properly utilized for improving the systems, structures and delivery of student services to the students.

Therefore, it is suggested that university should provide themes for such research, as are relevant and useful in improving different sub-systems and result cost-efficiency. Region specific and programme specific feedback/evaluation studies aimed at improving the student services should also be encouraged.

Contribution of research in improving the student support services in the University

The prime objective of researches in any system could be development and strengthening sub-systems involved in the system, those are primarily responsible for design, development, organization and management of its product and services. The same applies to distance education system as well because researches can play an important role in identification of cost-effective, cost-efficient innovative strategies and absorption of latest technologies in a viable manner for delivery of excellent quality of services to its students.

Respondents have opined that assessment of contribution made by research in development/ improvement of the learner services has not been done whereas one respondent has opined that researches undertaken are implemented for the advantage of the distance education system. Thus in the opinion of majority the, researches undertaken are not utilized for improving the quality of leaner services or development of systems.

It is suggested that university should consider some changes in its research funding policy like themes should be identified by the nodal agency, theme identification should be done carefully especially gray areas in the university system may be identified for this purpose. In addition, research studies should also extend on absorption of latest computer and communication technologies considering the viability aspect, obsoletion of technology. Finally, the outcome of the researches should be implemented for the system development. It will ensure utilization of resources spent towards research objectively.

Course of action on the research work undertaken at University

Majority of respondents are of the opinion that researches have been carried out in all the areas like materials the learning resources, services to the learners, student achievement, relevance and efficacy of learning in life and work situations, process and systems for developing and offering programmes and services and effective and efficient use of institutional systems, structures, materials and resources but findings of the researches are not available or published. It appears that adequate steps are not taken for identification of researches those can be implemented in the system. This shows that whatever researches undertaken are not used for improving its various sub-systems and activities and variables. This also shows that researches undertaken in the university are not contributing to the system, which is bad preposition and should not be allowed to continue.

Contribution of research in system improvement in the University

The university spends a lot of money towards promoting research with the objectives of improving the systems and services. The outcome of researches is to be implemented in the system for development/strengthening systems.

Respondents from the Academic Coordination Division have opined that research projects undertaken are not implemented for bringing improvement in the systems. This shows that resources allocated by the university towards research activities are not objectively utilized. As long as, the researches, which are undertaken with the objective of strengthening the systems and services are made use of for the purpose, the resources that are spent on the researches shall continue to waste. Therefore, it is suggested that outcome of researches must be implemented in the system for development of present systems, structures and strategies. Research plays a valuable role in continuous development of any system and same is the case with distance education system.

Implementation of research outcomes will prove beneficial in system improvement, which is a regular feature in present times.

Research projects undertaken by other academic departments in the University

Staff Training and Research Institute for Distance Education and Electronic Media Production Centre have also shown research as one of their objective, in addition to Academic Coordination Division.

However, the respondents from Staff Training and Research Institute for Distance Education and Electronic Media Production Centre have failed to provide the details of researches undertaken by the Centre. This means that STRIDE and EMPC do not undertake research and it has been just shown as their objective in the profile of the university. Moreover, launching/undertaking of research is the responsibility of the Academic Coordination Division as per the objectives laid down by the university. Therefore, it is suggested that there should be only one nodal agency responsible for management of research in Indira Gandhi National Open University. However, there should be a core group for identification of theme of researches to be undertaken, for evaluation of outcome of researches and for their implementation in the system. This will help research in contributing towards the development of systems and services of the university.

Outcome of programme evaluation and feedback studies undertaken in the University

Programme evaluation and feedback studies helps in knowing the strengths and weaknesses of the programme. Feedback on evaluative studies is useful in consolidation of programmes.

Majority of respondents from Planning and Development Division have indicated that they are not allowed to undertake feedback studies by the higher authorities in the division or university. This shows that enough studies on programme evaluation/system development and feedback are not undertaken for improving the various aspects related to delivery of student support services. It is a shocking revelation that attitude of the authorities is largely not conducive on matters related to system development as opined by respondents. Programme evaluation and feedback studies are of immense use in identification of gray areas and to take remedial measures.

Authorities in the university should encourage feedback and programme evaluation studies, which are crucial for development of programmes offered by the university. Feedback studies also point out the gray areas if any and are immensely helpful in changing strategies on various aspects of programme delivery.

Suggestions for strengthening research in the University

Following suggestion have been made by the respondents to improve the research function:

- Action research should be promoted in the system for bringing all around development in the distance education system.
- The research in the different sub-systems for strengthening their roles and activities is also need of the hour. The studies on cost-benefit analysis will also result in the cost-efficiency in the systems in distance education in the country.
- The researches undertaken and their outcomes should also be published for wider advantage of distance education in the country.

The research can play a crucial role in strengthening and development of distance education system provided researches undertaken are aimed at system improvement, programme evaluation and identification of judicious mix of different kind of media used in the system. Finally, researches on absorption and convergence of latest developments in the field of communication and computer technologies to the advantage of distance education are the need of the hour. Technologies are useful in providing uniform quality of product and services to one and all, and also help in reducing the over reliance on manpower, bringing cost-effectiveness and efficiency in distance education system.

Chapter 8

MANAGEMENT OF NETWORK OF STUDENT SERVICES AT IGNOU

In a distance education system students have to be provided with a wide range of services. In simple terms, these services include access to information about programmes, courses, how and when to enroll, whom to contact for tutorial guidance and advice, where to pay fees and where to sit for examinations and so on. Unlike the traditional system, in which the students generally have uniform levels of attainment, motivation and commitment, the open learning system usually has a vastly heterogeneous body of students. They are from diverse backgrounds, with varying levels of prior educational attainments, and their objectives are vastly different to fit any single pattern of attitudes, and behaviour. The managers of the open learning system have therefore to take all these factors into account while designing and organizing the student services sub-systems[60].

In establishing the student services systems in distance education, there are several concerns, which have to be taken into account. They are: [61]

- Vastness of the country and varying patterns and levels of educational development in different regions;
- Establishing the credibility of the distance education system in the context of the none too satisfactory experience with correspondence education;
- Securing the involvement of the vast educational infrastructure already available in the country in the promotion of distance education;

- Providing easy access to information, materials and services to the students.

The system of student services in distance education can be categorized into four major sub-systems as follows:

1. Student Registration and Database Sub-System
2. Material Distribution Sub-System
3. Student Support Services Sub-System
4. Student Assessment and Evaluation Sub-System

All these four functions taken together form network of student services. The success of any distance education system ultimately depends upon the effective functioning of network of student services systems. These activities as performed and managed at IGNOU are described and appraised in the following section of this chapter.

MANAGEMENT OF STUDENT REGISTRATION AND DATABASE SYSTEMS AT IGNOU

Student registration is concerned with timely advertisement, supply of forms, their collection, screening, and allotment of enrolment number, data entry, and communication of registration to students. Management of student registration, however, goes beyond these obvious functions. A responsible and committed institution needs to advertise widely, provide all kinds of pre-enrolment information, and render advise on different aspects. These include appropriateness of a programme in relation to student's needs, arrangements for effective and regular studies (including time scheduling), career prospects, the process of distance learning, cost, possible sources of financial support, nature of the certificate, diploma or degree and the like. Special care has to be taken, while designing the admission form cum prospectus, as it should be able to provide all information that the student needs as well as able to give adequate information that the institution requires. It should be easy to fill, and not too long. Effective management is one that ensures that information is updated regularly and made available to the students easily through brochures and advertisements; and over the phone, internet, radio or television.[62]

Besides effective management of student registration in any distance education institution, the timely, accurate and correct flow of information is also important for the decision making process which in turn is essential for effective management. The information is a critical input for realistic and accurate planning that requires continuous flow of information to all segments that need to plan the system and generate necessary resources to support the development in the system. Database Management System in any distance education system is required to maintain the data on programmes, courses, students, finances, counsellors, coordinators, staff, materials, inventory control, library acquisitions etc. Every system in the institution should have easy and quick access to relevant information, for which an effective MIS as sub-system of Database Management System must be managed effectively in any distance education institution.

Student Registration at IGNOU

Student Registration and Evaluation Division look after student registration functions at IGNOU while Database Management System is the responsibility of Computer Division. But due to internal reasons, the responsibility of student data was shifted to Student Registration and Evaluation Division.

Advertisement

The university is a national open university and its jurisdiction is all over the country. Therefore, it is must that information regarding commencement of admission reaches nook and corner of the country.

The academic year of the university starts on 1st January and 1 July (for Certificate and Management programmes only). This is done to provide opportunity to those who could not get admission in the conventional education system.

Majority of respondents from Student Registration and Evaluation Division have indicated that information regarding commencement of admission reaches all over the country through newspapers by way of advertisements in national and local dailies, through telecast on educational channel and broadcast on radio. In addition to this, Regional Centres also make local arrangements for wider publicity regarding commencement of admissions of the university like regional newspapers, cable TV and distribution of handout through learner support centres. Advertisement widely appears in the month of March/April every year for the academic cycle that starts from 1st January next year. This shows that university takes due care in ensuring that information reaches every corner of the country. This also helps the university in reaching the un-reached areas and making people in rural and remote areas aware about the educational programmes offered by Indira Gandhi National Open University for advancement of learning.

Sale and Receipt of Admission Forms Cum Prospectus

Admission forms cum prospectus for all the programmes offered by the university are available at the Regional and Learner Support Centres. However, filled in forms along with fees and testimonials are received at the Regional Centres, which are responsible for carrying out admissions. The forms for the programmes, having entrance examinations like management, information technology are received at Student Registration and Evaluation Division. However, admission forms for B.Ed. are received at the Regional Centres itself.

The university should have a uniform policy for receipt of admission forms for all the programmes and it should not be changed often. It is suggested that admission forms for all the programmes having entrance tests should also be received at the Regional Centres only. However, they should transmit all the details to Database Management System for further use like issuance of hall tickets, and making necessary arrangements for holding the entrance tests etc. This will help in complete decentralization of admission work to the Regional Centres; however, adequate manpower support to the Regional Centres should be ensured. It will be convenient for the aspiring students to approach the Regional Centres for issue of hall tickets or change of examination centre etc. Delegation of adequate powers to Regional Centres in this regard will also help in improving the student support system of the university.

The B.Ed., programme is in great demand and use of unfair means for getting the admission cannot be totally ruled out. Therefore, it is suggested all application received at the Regional Centres should be scrutinized and the candidates fulfilling prescribed conditions only be allowed to appear in the entrance tests.

Screening of application forms for admission

University has adopted different strategies for registration of students for its programmes. University conducts entrance test for its four programmes i.e., Management, Bachelor of Education, Bachelor of Information Technology and Advance Diploma in Information Technology; however, number of seats at each learner support centre in a region are fixed for B.Ed. programme, whereas, authorities decide the cut of point for Management, Bachelor of Information Technology and Advance Diploma in Information Technology every year. In some of the programmes like B. Sc. (Nursing) and Post Graduate Diploma in Maternal and Child Health number of seats under each Regional Centre are fixed and admissions are carried out by Regional Centres on merit basis. The university offers admission to all the eligible candidates in its remaining programmes, as there are no seat limits. The university has maximum enrolment in its computer programmes, which requires additional infrastructure facilities in form of computer institutes, qualified academic counsellors to meet the demand.

The respondents from Student Registration and Evaluation Division have indicated following mechanism for deciding the cut off point:

- Intake capacity for the academic year subject to securing minimum pass marks, which is 50% score.

- It is decided by a Committee appointed by the Vice-Chancellor and is kept secret but the objective is to maximize the enrolment with relaxed standards.
- In some programmes like B.Ed., criteria are merit based and eligibility as the number of seats is fixed.

The varied responses from the respondents indicate towards lack of knowledge on crucial policy matters. Therefore, it is suggested that training programmes on policy matters, rules and regulations should be organized for the personnel working in Student Registration and Evaluation Division for improving their knowledge, skills and competencies from time to time.

Respondents from Student Registration and Evaluation Division have also opined that results of entrance tests are processed within the division at present. But, fact is that outside agencies are involved in the process even when university has good computers and computer professionals to carry out this work. This will ensure sanctity of work and efficient utilization of resources at its disposal.

Majority of respondents from Student Registration and Evaluation Division have stated that every application received for admission at the Regional Centre go through two-tier scrutiny for ensuring that admission is in accordance with laid down rules. Respondents have also stated that admissions have been decentralized and it is the responsibility of the Regional Centres. However, the data received from the Regional Centres is verified through error checking software at Student Registration and Evaluation Division for ensuring that the admissions carried out are as per rules.

It is difficult for Regional Centres to carry out two-tier scrutiny of admission forms due to scarcity of manpower. At present more than 200 posts pertaining to Regional Centres in different cadres are lying vacant. Despite this, Regional Centres make their best efforts for ensuring the laid down criteria but human error is always a possibility. Error-checking software only point out the errors, which can be rectified at a later stage. But software cannot identify the deliberate errors in the admissions, if any. Therefore, it is better if Regional Centres are provided with the error checking software so that only error-free admission data is sent to the Student Registration and Evaluation Division. They should enforce strict regulations for ensuring that deliberate errors like favouritism etc., do not take place. Presently, the possibilities of such instances, cannot be completely ruled out, in the admission process.

The 2nd cycle of admission further adds to the hardship of the Regional Centres because as they do not have adequate manpower to carry out admissions even for 1st cycle. Majority of Regional Centres have to manage the admission work with the help of daily wagers and contract appointments, which lack competency and knowledge of admission work. Initially admissions were carried out once a year. Now university has introduced 2nd cycle of admission for its certificate programmes without providing additional/sufficient manpower to the Regional Centres. It is suggested that university should withdraw 2nd admission cycle or provide sufficient manpower to cope up with additional work to the Division and Regional Centres.

It is a fact that the students who join in January cycle of Bachelor of Preparatory Programme and Certificate in Computing have to waste six months in moving to Bachelor of Arts and Commerce and Bachelor of Computer Applications and Master of Computer Application. The admission process of the university is lengthy and results in wastage of more than six months period of students in comparison to conventional educational system and even in correspondence education programmes of the conventional universities and Distance Teaching Institutes in the country.

Therefore, university while designing policies on admissions should bear in mind that its admissions process do not result wastage of students precious time. Immediate efforts should be made to improve the present situation that results in loss of time to student fraternity.

Opinion of students towards the admission process of IGNOU

In order to have the perception towards admission process of the university, students were asked about the guidelines given in the student's handbook cum prospectus by the university with regard to clarity of guidelines as well as complete details about the programme to the learners. The opinion of all the 307 student respondents is shown in Table 15 below:

Table 15

Opinion of students towards admission process

	No. of Respondents			
	Yes	*No*	*No Response*	*Total*
Clear guidelines for admission	146 (47.55)	115 (37.46)	46 (14.99)	307
Complete details about the programme in prospectus	181 (58.95)	90 (29.31)	36 (11.74)	307

Source: Based on responses of students.

Majority of students 47.55% find the communication received from the university was clear but 37.46% students do not find the communication clear. University should make all efforts to use simple language and vocabulary in the admission form cum prospectus so that students understand the provisions and guidelines given in the student's handbook cum prospectus otherwise it affects their studies. Even though university brings out the admission form cum-prospectus in English and Hindi both, however, efforts should be made to make it understandable to the students keeping their level of education and knowledge standards in mind.

Majority of 58.95% students feel that students handbook cum prospectus provides complete information about the programmes of the university. Student's handbook cum-prospectus provides complete details of its admission process, course curriculum, and evaluation methodology and examination system in detail. Normally the conventional universities fail to provide all such details in their prospectus. However, Open University is practicing a different education system hence, it is essential to make students understand the provisions and guidelines in the admission form. However, every effort should be made to provide all the details in the prospectus so that applicants understand all the provisions easily. The university should consider bringing a separate student handbook cum prospectus for undergraduates, postgraduates and doctrate level programmes like management and B.Ed. etc. as the level of knowledge and understanding vary from student to student.

Database Management System at IGNOU

Regional Centres in the university carry out admission whereas Student Registration and Evaluation Division maintains consolidated master data of the admitted students centrally.

On enquiry, it was found that responsibility of maintenance of database was initially assigned to Computer Division. Computer Division in the university provides facilities like Internet, networking and pooled printing facilities and acquisition of computers in the university.

Respondents from the Computer Division have provided details about the computers installed and software developed by the division in the last four years, which is depicted in Table 16.

Table 16

Computers installed and Software Developed in the University

Year	*No. of Computers installed*	*No. of Software developed*
1998	250	2
1999	-	-
2000	500	3
2001	800	2

Source: Based on the responses from Computer Division.

It is surprising to note that despite having adequate number of computers, the university has not computerized all the sub-systems. The university should computerize its sub-systems in a planned manner. The acquisition of computers should have back support of software development+ for meeting the needs of different sub-systems.

A centralized database management system appears to be the key for distance education system. Database Management System will reduce the over procurement of computers and result in efficient utilization of technology acquired and also save the valuable resource by bringing effective coordination and communication among the sub-system of the university. It will also reduce the manpower needs of the university.

Majority of respondents from Student Registration and Evaluation Division feel that admission data is maintained systematically. But it is also correct that due to error or non-

+ Procurement of latest software is quiet fast but software development and on the job training in the university is in a bad shape and manpower resources are not optimally utilized for this purpose. The software development for strengthening the systems in the university is utmost important, this will result in accuracy, timely achievement of activities and require less efforts and manpower to carry out functions. This will also help in strengthening systems process in the system of the university.

existence of data a large group of students do not receive their study material.+

Management Information System at IGNOU

The data helps in evaluation of internal efficiency and effectiveness of each sub-system in the university. This data is a critical factor for assessment of each sub-system in the university system. Database Management System helps in timely organization of activities and effective control on organization of activities through Management Information System. ++

Majority of respondents from Planning and Development Division have clearly opined that MIS designed by project control unit, of the division is not adhered to by sub-systems in the university. MIS facilitates decision-making process by providing the status of activities on day-to-day basis and helps in close monitoring of activities in different sub-systems resulting improved coordination in the university.

The maintenance of a large data+++ should be on the principles of database management system. In such a large system, management of database should be a separate system in the university as planned initially. University has a large amount of student data, examination data, assignment evaluation data, evaluator's data, and invigilators data. Similarly, many other kinds of data for different other systems are also required to be maintained. All the data management should be entrusted to separate division/system in the university.

\+ Students are not receiving study material regularly. Please see Table 17 on page141.

++ Management information system is an integrated technique for gathering relevant information from whatsoever source it originates and transferring it into usable form for the decision making process.

+++ Different units of the university has to deal with a lot of data generated every day by the different sub-systems of the university, which has to coordinate data information generated by 7 Lac students, 23,000 academic counsellors, full time and part time staff around 5,000.

Initially, university functioned on the principles of database management system and its Computer Division was the nodal agency for this purpose. Presently, each sub-system is maintaining its own data and integration of database results in error, omissions, deletions etc. Therefore, it is suggested that an integrated database management system once again be introduced in the university to facilitate different user systems. This will help indirect transmission of admission, examination and assignment data from the Regional Centres to the database management system.

Database Management System will help the university in following:

- Realistic and accurate planning and selection of appropriate strategy;
- Control on admission processes and provision of materials and services accordingly;
- Control on timely production, distribution of materials and maintenance of quality and efficient utilization;
- Control on timely procurement of stores;
- Control on revenue collection and expenditure.

The database management system in the university will strengthen management information system, make quick transfer of data, possible and provide simultaneous access to all user sub-systems in the university.

Appropriate restrictions on its access to other sub-system users like modification he placed for maintaining security and accuracy of data, however, respective system users can modify data as per their need. In this system, each sub-system is responsible for purity of its data, working to a data entry schedule at university level. Each sub-system should be made accountable for the accuracy and ensuring updations from time to time and its performance in the achievement of goal would be open to general scrutiny.

MANAGEMENT OF MATERIAL DISTRIBUTION SYSTEM AT IGNOU

In distance education system, study material plays a vital role in supplementing face-to-face interface between the learner and teacher as study material is designed and developed on the principles of distance teaching-learning methodology, which helps learner in easy understanding of the subject matter and self test exercises helps in self evaluation to the learner.

The print materials received from the press or studio are to be properly stored in a manner that will allow for speedy verification of stock and retrieval for despatch. Stock verification and inventory control are crucial functions that must be undertaken with utmost care. As regards despatch decision has to be taken regarding mode of distribution (from a central warehouse or from regional centres or directly from the printers) and the periodicity of despatch. A time frame has to be fixed keeping in view the fact that the material reaches the learner via regional centres, learner support centres. The distribution may require booklet-wise (block-wise) packing or course-wise packing. The latter need to be handled professionally so as to reach the destination in time and good condition. Maintenance of computer based record, generation of address labels, their attachment to packages and recording despatch are examples of activities that have to be supervised carefully.[63]

Material delivery system at IGNOU

Delivery of instructional material to the students comprising self-instructional materials, assignments, programme guides, prospectus/handbooks is the responsibility of Material Production and Distribution Division (MPDD) of IGNOU. It also undertakes the activity of synchronization (course and medium wise) of production of material/ assignments, printing the required number of these materials, storing and despatching it to students, Regional Centres, Learner Support Centres throughout the country, thereby contributing to the student support services of the University.

This division is also responsible for the safe custody of all positives of course material in the University. It fixes the rates for each course material produced by the University. This unit also provides technical consultancy and advice to different Schools and Divisions. The stores of the division maintain the inventory of the quantity of study material required for students, sale and other purposes.[64]

The marketing cell[65] is responsible for the sale and promotion of the study material of the University. To achieve its objectives, it undertakes following functions:

- Sale of study material to general public especially through spot sale at headquarters;
- Sale of study material to universities/educational institutions in India and abroad;
- Appointing Retail Agents thereby enlarging the market for sale of study material;
- Participation in book fairs and exhibitions and sale of study material thereof;
- Undertaking promotional activities for popularizing the study material of the University through leaflets/ pamphlets etc.

Printing of study material at IGNOU

Schools provide with camera-ready copy of the study material for printing of study material for their courses. These copies can be preserved for re-printing. The university has created a bank of camera-ready copy at Material Production and Distribution Division but printing is the sole responsibility of the Schools presently and Material Production and Distribution Division has no role in printing of study material and assignments. The prerequisite for timely delivery of study material is timely printing of material for all the programmes.

Therefore, it is suggested that forecasting for printing of study material and assignments should start much before commencement of the admissions to avoid delay in despatch of study material and assignments to students, printing orders be placed in advance or beforehand. Forecasting accurately about the quantity to be printed in each case is of great value in terms of resources and to avoid wasting resulting out of surplus or excessive forcasting. Hence, it must be done with utmost care. The design, development and adherence to MIS in the university will prove beneficial in timely despatch of study material to the students.

In addition to timely delivery of study material to the students quality of print material should be of high order that facilitates reading. Language should be simple and easy to comprehend. Material Distribution Division should use good quality of packing material for safe delivery of study material to students by post. All the respondents of MPDD have suggested following steps to understand the contents:

- Use of good quality of paper;
- Standardization of pattern of printing and number of colours to be used;
- Coordination among different units and stores;
- Empanelment of quality printers;
- Use of standardized codes for each course and programme.

Other aspects involved in quality of study material are proper use of graphics and designs, proper editing for minimization of printing errors in material.

Inventory management for storage of paper and study material

The division also keeps stock of paper and printed material that needs proper storing and inventory management. The lack of inventory management system may result in misuse and wastage/loss of paper and study material.

Majority of respondents from Material Production and Distribution Division are of the opinion that inventory system for paper and print material is at present maintained manually by the division. The university has large inventory of paper and study material as it has launched more than 64 programmes having about 700 courses. It is, thus difficult to maintain the inventory of such a large print material manually. Apart from study material and assignments, MPDD also maintains inventory of other publications and papers. Therefore, it is suggested that division computerises inventory management system for proper organization and management of inventories without much delay. Computerized inventory maintenance will help in proper accounting of stores of study material and paper as well as maintenance of course-wise, programme-wise, inventory of study material, assignments, programmes guides etc.

Majority of respondents have opined that there exists sufficient and proper storage capacities for bulk paper in the division. But some respondents feel the need for additional storage capacity to meet the increased storage load of paper and print material. Proper storage is equally essential for proper inventory management; otherwise, it will result in wastage and deterioration of quality of paper, which may further result in poor quality of print material to the students. Paper and study material are valuable items procured by the university after investment of its valuable resources. Hence, it is essential to have proper storage facilities and adequate storage capacity with the division.

Insurance and safety measures

The huge storage of study material and paper. Workers involved in despatch of study material are not much educated and also have no proper training. The smoking etc. should be strictly prohibited otherwise it may become convenient source of fire. There is every possibility of the stock catching fire. Therefore, precautionary safety measures like installation of firefighting equipment is essential. Similarly, it is also essential to have all the stock of paper and study material insured being prone to fire and mutilation. The university has an inventory of crores of rupees stocked in the warehouses in the form of study material, paper and other publications. An incidence of fire may result in huge loss to the university.

Scheduling of despatch of study material and assignments

Preparation of despatch schedule in advance helps in timely despatch of study material and assignments to the students. Despatch schedule of division should form part of MIS of the university so that it helps in close monitoring of despatch of study material to students by higher authorities.

Respondents from MPDD have stated that following factors are considered in preparation of despatch schedule:

- Availability of stocks, ascending registration and total time required for despatch of study material keeping the last date of previous semester as target date;
- Time taken in compiling inventories, getting the print material, time taken by Student Registration and Evaluation Division in providing the detailed student registration and time taken by post offices to deliver the study material;
- To despatch the study material in time to the students.

All the respondents from MPDD are of the opinion that despatch schedule is prepared for timely despatch of study material to the students. The delay in receipt of study material by students shows that either the schedule prepared is not realistic or it is not strictly adhered while sending study material to the students.

In addition to above, the strategies for despatch of study material, manpower support for despatch of study material, and realistic scheduling should form part of scheduling for despatch of study material.

Despatch of study material and assignments

This division is primarily responsible for despatch of lakhs of packets of study material and assignments in each semester and it is very arduous and tedious task. The study material needs labeling before despatch, which is done by daily wagers who have little knowledge about the purpose and its importance. + From the responses of students, it has been observed that about 40% students do not receive the study material regularly and in time. The major reason for this is typographical errors in feeding the data for generating address labels.

There are thousands students to whom study material is not sent in time either due to deletion of records or various functional reasons like various types of errors that take place in feeding the data. At times, students also fail to fill up correct details in re-registration form. Another reason for non-receipt of study material is non-availability of the person/ recipient at the address to collect the study material, which is sent, by the university through registered post.

Table 17

Opinion of Students, Regional Centre and Learner Support Centres Towards Timely Delivery of Study Material and Assignments

	Regular and timely delivery of study material and assignments			
Respondents	*Yes*	*No*	*No Response*	
Students	144 (46.90)	138 (44.95)	25 (8.15)	307
Regional Centres	28 (50.90)	27 (49.10)	-	55
Learner Support Centres	55 (52.38)	48 (45.71)	2 (1.91)	105

Source: Based on the responses of students, respondents from Regional and Learner Support Centres.

\+ Student Registration and Evaluation Division provides data of students to whom study material is to be sent and indirectly plays a crucial role in despatch of study material. Records of students after finalization/ compilation of admission data received from the Regional Centres is passed on to the Material Distribution Division by SR&E. Time taken at SR&E in finalization of admission is of crucial importance. The delay in transmission of admission records results in delayed despatch of study material.

In Table 17 students by majority of 44.95% have denied timely and regular receipt of study material. Similarly, 49.10% respondents from Regional Centres have also opined against timely receipt of study material, endorsing the student's opinion. Similarly, 45.71% Coordinators (majority) have opined that Learner Support Centres do not receive study material for the programmes activated at their Centres.

Study material in distance education system is the primary mode of teaching- learning. It is essential for the university to ensure timely and regular supply of study material to students so that they do well in their studies in distance education system and their confidence in distance education is also strengthened. Study material is equally essential at the learner support centres as counsellors usually refer the study material before taking counselling session. In the absence of study material the quality of counselling cannot be expected to be satisfactory. The response of respondents from the Regional Centres is equally discouraging on timely supply of study material to students. Academics at the Regional Centres frequently refer the study material and programme guides to advise and counsel the students.

University should make sincere efforts to strengthen the timely and regular supply of study material, programme guide and assignments to the students so that they do not face any hardship while studying at the university. Learner Support Centres should also be provided with minimum 5 sets of study material as a policy of the university for the programmes activated at the centre and also supply the assignments regularly for use and reference by academic counsellors and students. Similarly, Regional Centres should be supplied study material and programme guides for all the programmes launched by the university in sufficient number. Material Production and Distribution Division should also ensure regular supply of assignments for each semester to the Regional Centres and Learner Support centres for meeting students need in the regions.

Suggestions for Improving the Performance of MPDD

The respondents from MPDD have suggested following steps for improving the performance of the Division:

- Proper monitoring of the plan of the division;
- Proper coordination with Schools and Division in the university;
- Timely submission of admission data by Student Registration and Evaluation Division;
- More staff for quality assurance and cost-effectiveness;
- Computerization of inventory management and
- More manpower to carry out the massive operation.

In addition to above suggestions, university should consider decentralization of distribution of study material to the Regional Centres, which will help timely delivery of study material to the students. All the students who personally submit their admission form at Regional Centres can be provided the study material same time resulting cost-effectiveness and efficiency both. Decentralization of distribution of study material to Regional Centres will improve student's access, in case of non-receipt of study material, they are easily acessible being close to the students in comparison to Material Production and Distribution Division, which is located in Delhi. It will also help in reducing the number of errors, which occur in transmission of data to Student Registration and Evaluation Division.

MANAGEMENT OF STUDENT SUPPORT SERVICES AT IGNOU

The management of student support services that involves complex system of education delivery to its learners is an uphill task in distance education system. The distance education institutes are using the networks consisting of Regional Centres and Learner Support Centres. Learner Support Centres include different kind of delivery channels depending upon the need of the programme and strategy to reach the students even in un-reached areas. The numbers of such centres depend upon the need of the learners and geography of that area.

The student support services sub-system is probably the most difficult sub-system to manage. This is because of the spatial separation of different units and facilities; and the considerable diversity in the categories of personnel involved. These include coordinators, programme in -charge, counsellors, tutors and line managers and periphery staff of Learner Support Centres and staff at Regional Centres. The counsellors, who constitute the long-standing staff at Learner Support Centres, provide counselling, tutorial and evaluation support to the students. The tutor, who is subject expert, provides resource materials, gives feedback on assignments, advises on personal and career problems, and generally encourages the students. Coordinator at the Learner Support Centre is responsible for looking after the tutorial services at the grass-root level. The staff at the Regional Centre, headed by the Regional Director, plays the crucial role in monitoring the functioning of the Learner Support Centres. It provides feedback to headquarters and relays back advice and instruction to the centres. The management of these personnel, who must work in coordination, requires skill, tact and patience.[66]

Student Support Services System at IGNOU

The function of student support services system at IGNOU is a three- tier system consisting of Regional Services Division, Regional Centres and Learner Support Centres. (Refer to Figure 3)

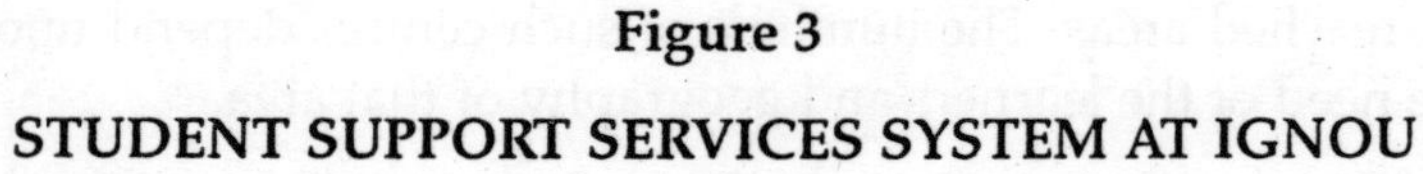

Figure 3

STUDENT SUPPORT SERVICES SYSTEM AT IGNOU

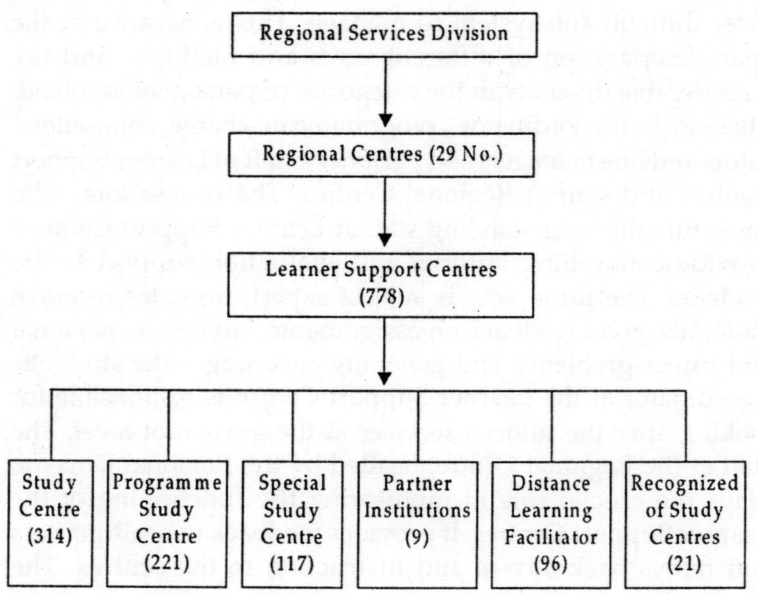

Source: Database, Regional Services Division, IGNOU

The Regional Services Division[67] in IGNOU located at New Delhi is responsible for implementing the objectives of the University. This division is responsible for providing academic, administrative and informative support to learners through various contact channels to break isolation. The responsibilities of the Regional Services Division are following:

1. Establishment of Regional Centres and Learner Support Centres;
2. Design, develop delivery schemes for delivery of student support services;
3. Formulate policies, systems and procedures for management of Regional and Learner Support Centres;

4. To provide manpower and infrastructure support to Regional and Learner Support Centres;
5. Appointment and renewal of Coordinators and Programme In charge;
6. Appointment and Renewal of Academic Counsellors;
7. Programme activation;
8. Coordination with Schools and Divisions at the headquarters;
9. Monitoring of activities of Regional and Learner Support Centres and sharing feedback;
10. Funding and expenditure control over Regional and Learner Support Centres;

Regional Centre at IGNOU

Regional Centre has to play an important and crucial role in creation and management of network of learner support centres by ensuring efficient and effective delivery of student services. This requires excellent organization, coordination, and managerial skills to manage the affairs of the learner support centres in the region successfully.

Regional Centres are established by university for the purpose of coordinating and supervising delivery of student services through Learner Support Centres in any region and for promoting such other functions as may be conferred on such Centres by the Board of Management. Regional Centres, the sub-offices of the university for all practical purposes, are intended to act as resource centres of university in respective regions. Regional Centres are centres for training of Coordinators, Counsellors, and other part-time functionaries. Presently, there are 23 Regional Centres of the University and 6 Regional Centres are functioning under North-East Project. The responsibilities entrusted to Regional Centres at present are indicated in Table 18.

Table 18

Functions of Regional Centres

Admissions	Identification of Learner Support Centres
Appointment and renewal of Coordinators	Monitoring of Learner Support Centres
Appointment and renewal of Academic Counsellors	Coordination with Schools and Divisions
Management of Regional and Learner Support Centres	Library facilities at Regional and Learner Support Centres
Interactive Radio Counselling	Conduct of Term-end-examination
Teleconferencing	Convocation

Learner Support Centres

The Learner Support Centres form an important part of overall structure of the university designed to provide extensive and efficient student support services to its learners. These are established to offer students a 'Kit of Communication Channels' to supplement the contents of the course in the form of print material mailed to them and enable them to interact with academic counsellors and fellow students as also to provide access to modern technology through the use of audio-video aids and teleconferencing. It seeks to help students in independent learning by means of appropriate forms of educational technologies. IGNOU has following six types of Learner Support Centres [68]:

(i) Study Centres

These centres offer most of the programmes of IGNOU and are located in those host institutions, which provide rent free accommodation. The university provides furniture and equipment to facilitate multi-media teaching and bears all recurring and non-recurring expenditure.

(ii) Programme–Study Centre

A centre established for providing necessary student support services for a particular programme (Science, Technology, Engineering, Computers, Health Sciences, Library and information and professional/vocational which have intensive practical component) is called a programme study centre.

(iii) Special Study Centre

A centre located in an institution/organization like non-governmental organization (NGO's), Voluntary Organizations, Panchayats, Cooperatives or Government departments and public institutions dedicated to the cause of a given disadvantaged group. Under this scheme, university shares a fix part of fees on per student basis.

(iv) Partner Institutions

It is a scheme to draw upon the existing resources already available with various organizations and institutions for effective delivery of its programmes. Partnership arrangements have been made to supplement the IGNOU's programme delivery mechanism. The university shares a fix percentage of fees on per student bases.

(v) Distance Learning Facilitator

It is a one man scheme to provide support services to the students in the areas not having institution-based support facilities, area-specific persons, who may be retired teachers/officers, professionals, house-wives, motivated individual(s) even if unemployed, and having a post graduate degree and permanently residing in the given area, are empanelled as Distance Learning Facilitator.

(vi) Recognized Study Centre

Recognized study centres are run with the support and involvement of government undertakings, voluntary organizations and other institutions interested in promoting open learning system. The host institutions provide rent-free accommodation, furniture and equipment and also meet the expenditure on counselling.

Primary functions of a Learner Support Centre are shown in Table 19.

Table 19

Functions of Learner Support Centres

Identification of Academic Counsellors	Management of Learner Support Centres
Organization of counselling/ practical session	Organization of audio-video sessions
Timely evaluation of assignments and feedback	Liaison with academic institutions, experts and scholars
Maintenance of accounts	Appointment of part-time staff
Conduct of term-end-examination	Dissemination of information to prospective and present students

Establishment of Regional Centre at IGNOU

Majority of respondents from Regional Services Division have opined that following factors are taken into consideration while opening Regional Centres:

- Student enrolment and black hole districts;
- Need of particular area, number of learner support centres;
- Budgetary provisions, need of a region and student enrolment.

The university has been deciding well in advance for the establishment of Regional Centre up till VIII Five year Plan. However, during IXth plan period Regional Centres were established at Jammu, Srinagar, Ghaziabad (later shifted to Dehradun), Ranchi and Khanna without any systematic planning. University normally establishes one Regional Centre in a State. But in case of J&K two Regional Centres have been established at Jammu and Srinagar even though the student enrolment at Regional Centre, Jammu does make it a viable unit. Similarly, Regional Centre Shimla, Karnal, Khanna and Jammu have been established without considering the financial viability, as student enrolment is too low in these States. It would have been better to locate the Regional Centre ideally at Chandigarh to cater to the needs of students presently enrolled with Regional Centre Shimla, Khanna, Jammu and Karnal.

Similarly, university has established six Regional Centres in the North-Eastern States at Imphal, Gangtok, Itanagar, Tripura, Aizwal and Kohima despite the fact that even the existing two Regional Centres at Guwahati and Shillong are not viable. Till recently, its existing Regional Centres Guwahati and Shillong looked after all the North-Eastern States. The student enrolment combining all the eight Regional Centres of North-East may not be more than 5000.

Establishment of Regional Centres without proper planning puts additional financial burden on the university. On one hand, university is establishing Regional Centres in haste without proper planning and on the other hand it has completely failed to provide the sanctioned staff for the smooth functioning of existing Regional Centres . The staffing pattern itself was decided as back as in 1991. Thereafter, university has expanded manifold in terms of student enrolment, number of programmes, number of learner support centres. The pattern of staffing, therefore, needs to be reviewed otherwise its student support system may collapse.

University must provide adequate staff to all the Regional Centres for delivering quality services to the students. New Regional Centres should not be established unless there are sufficient staff to carry out the responsibilities of a Regional Centre well. It is suggested that university should also consider financial viability as an aspect before opening Regional Centre.

The university should devise a policy for establishment of Regional Centres instead of opening Regional Centres in a pick and choose manner.

Moreover, many States have established Open Universities in their States. Student enrolment in the Open Universities puts a question mark on the viability of establishing a State University or Regional Centre of Indira Gandhi National Open University for achieving the same objective as it results into double expenditure towards same activity.

Therefore, it is suggested that university should devise a policy for establishment of Regional Centres considering the changed scenario with coming up of State Open Universities. This assumes greater importance when IGNOU is also an apex body for promoting distance education system and maintenance of standards in distance education system in the country. State Open Universities also offer majority of programmes offered by Indira Gandhi National Open University. Alternative and innovative strategies needs to be identified for keeping the distance and open education system liable and cost efficient.

Design and Development of Learner Support Centres (Delivery Schemes) at IGNOU

Delivery of student services in distance education system is through delivery schemes. Delivery schemes play vital role at the field level in delivering student service through various modes like counselling, audio-video, teleconferencing, computers etc. Delivery channels are an in-built part of the programme development.

Majority of respondents from Regional Services Division are of the opinion that delivery schemes for student support services are developed considering, the need of students, financial viability, appropriateness for meeting the needs of the programmes delivery, available technology to broaden accessibility. All thse issues are discussed among group members in the division and further discussion with higher authorities and finally approval of Academic Council is obtained before its imlementation.

As per the concept of distance education, delivery mechanism is an in built part of programme design and development and it is the responsibility of concerned School to bring out an appropriate delivery mechanism after field tests considering various aspects of programme delivery i.e., academic, administrative and financial. The objective of delivery schemes should be to ensure efficient services to the students for better attainment. While designing programmes and delivery strategies the role and extent of each media should be kept in mind and accordingly print and media materials should be prepared.

Establishment of Learner Support Centres at IGNOU

Majority of respondents from Regional Services Division have stated that Learner Support Centres are area specific, programme specific for providing student support services to its students. In some cases, university provides furniture and equipment to Learner Support Centres and also meets the recurring and non-recurring expenditure. In some schemes of Learner Support Centres university shares fees in addition to payment of remuneration to the Coordinator/ Programme in charge for providing student support services to its students but does not provide furniture and equipment etc.

Every scheme envisages minimum student enrolment at each Learner Support Centre considering viability factor. As on date, university has more than 750 Learner Support Centres and enrolment at more than 100 centres is said to be less than 100. University incurs an expenditure of Rs.2.5 Lac towards providing furniture and equipment to a Learner Support Centre [Study Centres (314) and Special Study Centres (117)]. University also spends a minimum amount of Rs. 80,000/ and Rs. 28,000/- p.a. towards remuneration of coordinators and part-time functionaries at Study Centre and Special Study Centre respectively. Considering non-viability factor, it becomes a financial burden on the university.

Similarly, university has launched the scheme of Distance Learning Facilitator for providing student services in rural and remote areas in the country. But proper objectives, strategies for providing student services are not well defined in the scheme. Financial viability considering the utility of the scheme is also an important factor which needs to be looked into. University is spending a reasonable sum towards remuneration of Distance Learning Facilitators and administrative expenses on their selection process. This shows that the university has launched the delivery schemes without considering the need, viability and appropriateness of the schemes to facilitate the targeted learners.

Finally, merit should be the sole criteria behind establishment of Learner Support Centres otherwise their establishment results into wastage of financial resources. Therefore, university must test its various schemes launched for providing student support services to the students from administrative, academic and financial angle and consider viability and need factor while opening Learner Support Centres.

Manpower Support to Regional and Learner Support Centres

All the respondents from the Regional Services Division and Regional Centres have stated that manpower support to the Regional Centres is poor. However, manpower support to Learner Support Centres has been decentralized and delegated to the Regional Centres. There are norms for this purpose and part-time staffs are provided to the Learner Support Centres. This is working satisfactorily.

The university has completely failed in providing adequate/sanctioned manpower to its 29 Regional Centres. As on date, more than 200 posts at the Regional Centres are lying vacant. Majority of Regional Centres are finding it difficult to cope up with the quantum of work increasing day by day. Regional Centres are managing the work with the help of daily wagers and contract appointments as an ad-hoc arrangement. It is impossible to carry out the work with the help of daily wagers and contract appointments in an efficient manner. Moreover, there are restrictions on hiring the services of the same person after a period of time. It is very difficult to train a new person every time. It is suggested that university should take urgent steps for filling up the vacant posts and simultaneously review the staff strength, which was sanctioned way back in 1991. The absence of adequate staff affects the delivery of student support services and its monitoring in a region.

Infrastructure Support to Regional and Learner Support Centres

The next logical step after establishment of Regional and Learner Support Centres is providing them with adequate manpower and required furniture and equipment items and technological support to them.

Majority of respondents from Regional Services Division and Regional Centres have opined that infrastructure support provided by the university to Regional Centres is sufficient and adequate.

The university has devised norms for providing furniture and equipment support to Learner Support Centres (Study Centres and Special Study Centres only). Initially, university had supplied the furniture and equipment items as per the norms. There has been some problem for last 2-3 years as Regional Services Division has totally failed in providing furniture and equipment support to all the newly established Study Centres and to all the Special Study Centres (117). In absence of required furniture and equipment support these centres are not able to provide required audio-video and teleconferencing facilities to the students.

Therefore, it is suggested that all the established centres be provided with provisioned furniture and equipment so that student services do not suffer. Technology is the factor that distinguishes distance education system with correspondence education. Hence, all the Learner Support Centres should be provided with provisioned audio-video and teleconferencing facilities as per policy of the university as and when centres are established.

Appointment of Coordinators and Programme Incharge at the Learner Support Centres

Regional Centres send the proposal for appointment of coordinator/ programme incharge along with the proposal of opening Learner Support Centres, in accordance with the norms devised for the purpose. The proposal after their scrutiny at Regional Services Division sent to the Vice-Chancellor for approval/consideration. As per policy of the university appointment of condinater/Programme Incharge is valid for a period of one year, which is however, renewed every year for a maximum period of five years. In addition, appointments are made whenever there is change of person, on the recommendations of host institution etc. The policy of the university is flexible on appointment of coordinator/ programme-Incharge. It is expected that while sending the proposal for renewal of their term past performance is taken into consideration. But it is amazing that terms are renewed even when their past performance are not satisfactory and student enrolment is too low. Therefore, it is suggested that while renewing the term of coordinators, there past performance should be taken into account. Further, appointment of coordinators should be based on their past performance in terms of counselling/practical sessions organized, timely evaluation of assignments, organization of audio-video sessions etc.

In case of appointment of programme-incharge, the matter is referred to the School concerned for concurrence to ensure that person recommended is capable of handling the programme related delivery services at the centre as programme centres are programme specific.

Special Study Centres are established at NGO's, Voluntary Organizations, Block Development Offices and Gram Panchayats etc., with an objective to make the educational available in rural and remote areas. The person recommended for appointment as coordinator should be a Reader or equivalent. It is impossible for all these institutions to fulfill this condition. This shows that provisions made in the policies are not realistic and feasible. Hence, realistic and feasible provisions should be incorporated in the scheme and performance should be sole criteria for appointment and extensions of the term of coordinators. But it is amazing to note that coordinators are being appointed without fulfilling this condition and appropriate corrections in the policies are also not made.

Appointment and renewal of Academic Counsellors

Academic counsellors are appointed for counselling the students at Learner Support Centres. Each School has laid down guidelines for appointment of academic counsellors for their programmes. Accordingly, persons are identified by the learner support centres and their bio-data in the prescribed proforma are sent to the Regional Centres, which in turn send it to Regional Services Division. Regional Services Division sends it to concerned School for concurrence and thereafter appointment order is issued to the person.

From the above, it is clear that processes of appointment of academic counsellors are cumbersome as many channels are involved in it. Majority of respondents from Regional Services Division, Regional Centres and Learner Support Centres have stated that their exits provision for renewal of the term of academic counsellors but it has never happened. The authorities in the university should consider decentralization and delegation of powers for appointment and renewal of academic counsellors to the Regional Centres as it takes long time to issue appointment order to the concerned person. The misuse of delegated powers and defiance of guidelines should be strictly dealt with.

Regional Services Division is also finding it difficult to maintain the database of academic counsellors programme-wise, centre-wise, and region-wise. Either proper database should be maintained at the Division or as suggested earlier this responsibility should be entrusted to Database Management System so that availability of academic counsellors in sufficient number are ensured before launching or activation of programme.

Coordination of Regional Services Division with Schools and Divisions

Regional Services Division is mainly a coordinating Division, which facilitates its Regional and Learner Support Centres in smooth conduct of their activities. The division coordinates with Schools on launch of academic programmes and appointment of academic counsellors, with Schools and STRIDE on conduct of orientation/training programmes for academic counsellors to converse them with the teaching-learning methodology of distance education system, coordinators and part-time functionaries of the centres on administrative and financial management at the centres. Regional Services Division also coordinates with other divisions of university for providing various kinds of support to the Regional Centres as all the divisions are involved in facilitating student support services. This division also coordinates with Electronic Media Production Centre for conduct of teleconferencing and providing audio-video support to Regional and Learner Support Centres.

Respondents from Division, and Learner Support Centres have clearly stated that staff training and media support to the learner support centres in the university is very poor, which puts a question mark on coordination system of the division as it has totally failed in providing or strengthening the training and media support to the Regional and Learner Support Centres. Similarly, coordination with Schools is also not good as neither academic counsellors are appointed in time nor orientation and training programme are organized satisfactorily as about 50% academic counsellors taking counselling sessions at present are untrained. This adversely affects the quality of counselling to students and their enrichment. Had, the Regional Services Division pointed out all these matters in time to the concerned authorities in the university, the situation of the student support services of the university would have been exemplary.

It is clear that Regional Services Division has totally failed in coordinating the activities with Schools and Divisions that has adversely affected the performance of Regional and Learner Support Centres and quality of academic input to the students. This further indicates that higher authorities have equally failed in monitoring the responsibilities of such an important division. Functioning of Regional Services Division needs continuous monitoring by higher authorities to ensure timely and quality services to the students throughout the country.

Programme activation at the Learner Support Centres

Regional Services Division is also responsible for programme activation at the learner support centres. Majority of respondents from the Regional Services Division have stated that programme activation is based on the recommendation of Regional Directors who ensure availability of enough number of academics counsellors for all courses of a programme. In case of specialized programmes like computers, engineering, education etc., Regional Director ensures all the required facilities before recommending the activation of programme at a centre.

It is suggested that Regional Director be asked to submit bio-data of academic counsellors in sufficient number for all the courses of a programme for ensuring quality of academic counselling and practical inputs to the students. It is seen that sometimes, Regional Centres recommend programme activation at the centre without ensuring availability of sufficient academic counsellors and as a result, students attached to the centre face difficulties later. The process of programme activation should be standardized and Regional Centres should be instructed to send sufficient bio-data's for appointment of academic counsellors for all the courses of that programme. It will ensure availability of adequate counselling and practical facilities to the students at Learner Support Centres.

Monitoring of activities of Regional and Learner Support Centres

Regional Services division is responsible for monitoring the activities of Regional and Learner Support Centres. The university has expanded a lot during last decade in terms of Regional Centres, Learner Support Centres and student enrolment. To keep the systems in strengthened form and efficient, it is essential that extensive and continuous monitoring of activities of Regional and Learner Support Centres is carried out.

Majority of respondents from the Regional Services Division and Regional Centres have opined that monitoring system are ineffective. However, respondents from learner support centres have opined that monitoring is occasionally carried out. Regional Centres and Learner Support Centres do not send the prescribed monitoring reports* in time and whatever little reports are received in the division are not evaluated for providing feedback. Monitoring is a two-way mechanism that helps in strengthening the activities in any system. Monitoring system needs to be defined clearly and should be mandatory for all the Regional and Learner Support Centres. Proper feedback should also be provided on the monitoring reports so that centres can improve upon their performance.

Lack of monitoring has totally affected the delivery of student support services like audio-video services, teleconferencing services, and library facilities (The opinion of students, respondents from Regional and Learner Support Centres have been discussed in Table 12, 14 and 16 respectively in earlier discussions). Audit is an important tool for monitoring

---

* Regional Centres and Learner Support Centres are required to send monthly monitoring reports to Regional Services Division in the prescribed formats:

(i) Counselling
(ii) Practical
(iii) Audio-video sessions and
(iv) Assignment evaluation

the performance of Regional and Learner Support Centres. As a policy, there exists provision for audit of activities of Regional and Learner Support Centres. Internal audit system of university is so poor that activities of Learner Support Centres have rarely been audited.

Main reason for lack of monitoring of Learner Support Centres is shortage of adequate manpower at the Regional Centres as they find it difficult to coop up with the quantum of work in their hand. Whatever little monitoring is carried out is also put under the carpet and no action is initiated for the laxity and misuse on part of these centres.

Finally, it is suggested that first of all Regional Centres should be provided adequate manpower and effective monitoring mechanism should be developed and made systems process. Monitoring in distance education system can be categorized into two viz. activity monitoring and financial monitoring.

It is difficult to carry out academic monitoring of the activities performed by the learner support centres. The researcher has devised one monitoring proforma, a consolidated proforma for monitoring the activities of Learner Support Centres (Monthly feedback report for all the four activities). The new devised feedback proforma is shown as Exhibit III for carrying out activity monitoring. It should be made compulsory for all the Learner Support Centres to submit report on organization of counselling, practical, audio-video and evaluation of assignments during the month. The reasons for not being able to meet the target should be explicitly stated by the centre. Reports received from the Learner Support Centres should be analyzed by the Regional Centres for onward submission to the Regional Services Division. Finally, Regional Services Division should correlate the comments of Learner Support Centre and Regional Centre while evaluating the performance. At the end, feedback should be shared with the Learner Support Centre through Regional Centre. The feedback on activity monitoring should also be shared with concerned division/school at headquarters for taking remedial measures

In case monitoring reports from a Regional Centre in respect of Learner Support Centres in that region are not received in time, this should also be pointed out timely. If performance of a Learner Support Centre continues to be unsatisfactory, its closure should be recommend to the appropriate authority.

Student grievance handling mechanism at IGNOU

The university has a large and complex student delivery system across the length and breadth of the country. It is impossible to attain complete efficiency in every aspect of university functioning. Large democratic system demands an effective and faster redressal mechanism. Therefore, it is essential to have an effective redressal system of student grievances at the university.

Majority of respondents from Regional Services Division have stated that there exists a Student Welfare Centre at the headquarters and Student Affairs Cell for handling student grievances in the division. Student Welfare Centre was established three years ago in 1999; prior to which Student Affair Cell was looking after the student grievances that used to settle student grievances in close coordination with Divisions and Regional Centres.

Student Welfare Centre is very helpful in handling the student grievances. Student Welfare Centre being located in Delhi is able to redress the grievances of the students residing in and around Delhi as they are in a position to approach it personally. The Centre also attends to the student grievances received by post, but they do not get such a quick redressal. The majority of functions like material distribution, evaluation are centralized and in case of any problem student approaches headquarters either through their Regional Centre or individually but in that case mechanism is not that effective and purposeful.

It is suggested that the work of material distribution should be decentralization to the Regional Centres. Similarly, Regional Centres should be assigned the responsibility of consolidation of assignments grades from all the centres for the students in their region. This will facilitate quicker handling of student grievances related to assignment grades and non-receipt of study material. Thus students will be saved from the fatigue of running to headquarters at Delhi on issues, which constitute major part of student grievances. In addition, university should provide (WAN) wide area network facilities to all its Regional Centres so that same data can be accessed at Regional Centre itself and student's grievances are instantly redressed.

Conduct of counselling/practical at Learner Support Centres

The most important function of the Regional Services Division is organization of counselling and practical sessions for the students through Learner Support Centres. Basic purpose of opening Learner Support Centres is to provide academic input through various means like face-to-face counselling, practical facilities in case of science and technology programmes, assignment evaluation and feedback to students.[+] In addition to these, Learner Support Centres also provide audio-video and teleconferencing support to the students[++].

Majority of students and respondents from Regional Centres have opined that student attendance in counselling sessions is average. As per policy of the university 75% attendance in practical sessions for computer programmes is compulsory for appearing in the final (TEE) examinations. However, university has not devised any mechanism for it's monitoring and all the students who fill up examination form are normally allowed to appear in the term-end-examination. The provisions those are not possible to adhere should not be laid down as the policy. Some of Regional Centres have enforced it at their level and do not allow the students to sit in the practical examinations. To overcome this situation, students

---

[+] Assignment Evaluation is discussed in forthcoming discussion on pp. 164-176. (Assessment and Evaluation System)

[++] Audio-video and teleconferencing has been discussed in Chapter VI. (Media Systems)

mark fake attendance to appear in the practical examination. These fake attendances inflate the claim of these private institutions, which they charge from the university. Either university should strictly enforce the policy of 75% attendance uniformally by designing proper systems and procedures for its compliance or withdraw it, as it is proving costly for the university. It is sure that majority of students are availing the assignment evaluation facilities at the Learner Support Centres as it has weightage of 25-30% in qualifying the programme. Majority of respondents from Regional Centres have also opined that Learner Support Centres are finding it difficult to get qualified academic counsellors for computer courses and situation in rural and remote areas is more serious.

Suggestion for improving the performance of Student Support Services at IGNOU

Respondents from Regional Services Division, Regional Centres and Learner Support Centres were asked to make suggestions for the improvement of the performance of Regional Services Division, Regional Centres and Learner Support Centres respectively. Their suggestion are given below:

- Organizational restructuring be undertaken for effective and efficient coordination and communication systems. The structure of the university should be in pyramid form and headquarters should only concentrate on policy, planning, reviewing, resource allocation, audit, programme evaluation, student evaluation and research. All activities aimed at students are decentralized with adequate staff, commensurate delegation of powers for carrying out the responsibility of university towards students. Database Management Systems should be restructured for strengthening coordination and communication across the sub-systems in the university.
- The number of Regional Centres be reduced and each Regional Centre should have minimum 25,000

students and regions be defined in terms of student enrolment and not in terms of geographical boundaries like State or Union Territories.

- Similarly, establishment of Learner Support Centres should be need-based. As per as possible minimum 500 students should be allocated to each Learner Support Centres for making them viable for optimum utilization of resources.
- Technological support to the students must be ensured with its proper utilization to the advantage of students and technological developments should overcome human incapabilities.

Suggestion given by the respondents about providing of staff and introducing monitoring, as a systems process needs to be implemented without further delay. Decentralization of work and delegation of more powers, commensurate staff is the need of the hour. Similarly, training has to be a systematic process and orientation of part-time functionaries should be a regular feature for improving the performance and delivery of student services for their better attainment. Finally, all the procedures and systems are to be defined clearly resulting role clarity among the personnel in the university. The university has to ensure the efficient functioning of its Regional and Learner Support Centres to provide above par services to the students. Systems and process should be carefully planned and should also be followed religiously. To a greater extent, the image of the university is linked to the kind of services they deliver to the students, which is the ultimate objective of the university.

MANAGEMENT OF STUDENT ASSESSMENT AND EVALUATION SYSTEM AT IGNOU

In any distance education system, the institution providing academic programmes-services is also involved in the assessment of learners and management of processes of learner evaluation. This learner evaluation is done in two parts: 1)

Student assessment (Assignment Evaluation) and 2) Term-end-examination.

Assessment evaluation involves the marking and grading of assignments, providing advice in the form of comments, and speedy return of the graded material to the student. Casual correction, without meaningful comments and delay in return of assignments may lead to loss of interest and increase in no. of dropout. Hence, it is necessary to ensure that assignments are properly evaluated and for this, encouragement and motivation of the tutors is necessary.[69]

Procedure followed by open universities for conduct of term end examination, and the evaluation of answer-scripts, is similar to that of conventional universities. Management responsibilities are those related to secrecy in the setting of question papers, its proper moderation, fair conduct of examinations at the centres, the prompt despatch of answer-scripts to headquarters, appointment of competent examiners and prompt examination of answer-scripts. Subsequent steps are the tabulation of marks and declaration of results.[70]

Student assessment (assignment evaluation at IGNOU is done through Learner Support Centres, whereas the function of term-end-examination is looked after by Student Registration and Evaluation Division.

Student Registration and Evaluation Division[71] of IGNOU is mainly responsible with student assessment and evaluation. Major functions of this division are as follows:

- Monitoring registration of students for various programmes/courses;
- Evaluation of their performance in term-end-examinations held in June and December every year;
- Evaluation of computer marked assignments;
- Issue of hall tickets to the students appearing in the examinations;
- Issuing consolidated grade cards showing assignment and term-end grades to the students;

- Award of degrees, diplomas and certificates to the successful learners.

This division is the main repository of the students central database relating to course registration, assignment scores and term-end-examination scores.

Student assessment and evaluation methodology at IGNOU

Evaluation methodology adopted by the university is different from the conventional system of education like credit system, grading system and weightage to assignments and term-end examinations.

Performance of students at IGNOU is evaluated on the basis of assignments submitted by them, of term-end examination conducted at the end of expiry of minimum duration prescribed for the course/programme, execution of specific projects, field works, seminars, practicals or any other technique for assessment to determine the levels of performance of students pursuing different courses/programmes.

Majority of respondents from Student Registration and Evaluation Division have stated that evaluation methodology is made clear to the students at the start of the programme.

University provides the details of evaluation procedure for each programme in the programme-guide supplied to the students alongwith courseware. It is clearly stated in programme guide that university has semester system of examinations and tutor marked assignment, computer marked assignment, practicals, field works, projects and term-end examinations are given due weightage in overall evaluation system of the university.

Assignment evaluation at IGNOU

Teaching-learning methodology of distance education system uses tutor-mark-assignments as two-way communication system, which provides feedback to learners and is compulsory component of the evaluation system at

IGNOU. Assignments carry a weightage of 25-30% in overall assessment and as per present policy of the university, there should be one assignment for every two-credit course and maximum number of assignments for eight-credit course should not exceed three.

University uses three types of assignments viz.: Tutor Marked Assignments (TMA), Computer Marked Assignments (CMA) and Project Assignments. The assignment evaluation involves a number of academic and operational issues like designing of assignments, preparation and production of assignments, timely despatch to learners, despatch to Learner Support Centres and Regional Centres, assignment evaluation by academic counsellors, timely feedback to students after evaluation, timely despatch of grades/marks to the Student Registration and Evaluation Division, entry of assignment grades at headquarters by SR&E Division, entry of computer marked assignment grades by SR&E Division, monitoring of receipt of grades from learner support centres at SR& E Division.

The university also has a policy of random checking of 2% of assignments by the concerned faculty. This is an important aspect as it plays an important role in improving the quality of assignment evaluation and feedback to the students, which is however not being carried out by the teachers in the university. Authorities have failed in implementing the policy in letter and spirit. This shows that the university is not sincere about its objective of rendering quality services to the students.

Tutor Marked Assignments

Delivery of assignments to students is the responsibility of MPDD. (details about MPDD have been discussed earlier on pp 135-142). Respondents from Regional Centres and Learner Support Centres were asked with regard to receipt of timely feedback on assignments. Their responses are shown in Table 20.

Table 20

Opinion of Students, Regional Centre and Learner Support Centres towards timely feedback on Tutor Mark Assignments

Respondents	*Yes*	*No*	*No Response*	
Students	128 (41.69)	166 (54.07)	13 (4.24)	307
Regional Centres	25 (45.45)	29 (52.74)	1 (1.91)	55
Learner Support Centres	53 (50.48)	47 (44.76)	5 (4.76)	105

Source: Based on the responses of students, respondents from Regional and Learner Support Centres.

Majority of 54.07% student respondents have clearly stated that they do not receive timely feedback on tutor-mark assignments, which they submit at the learner support centres. Assignments are an integral component of teaching-learning methodology in distance education system and play an important role in student enrichment through timely feedback provided through assignments. Comments of academic counsellors provide desired feedback to the students through assignments, which play a crucial role in making them understand about their level of performance in their studies. Similarly, majority of 52.74% respondents from Regional Centres have also endorsed the viewpoint of students that timely feedback on assignments is not provided to them. Finally, 44.76% respondents from Learner Support Centres have also confirmed that there is undue delay in returning of evaluated assignments to students. Not only this, respondents have also opined that feedback on assignments fail to provide the desired feedback through assignments. This may be because most of the academic counsellors are not oriented/trained by the university for doing their work according to the needs and principles of distance education system. An untrained academic counsellor fails to understand the teaching-learning methodology of distance education and the important role he is expected to play in the form of providing feedback through tutor mark assignments.

Majority of respondents from Student Registration and Evaluation Division have stated that grades for evaluated assignments from the learner support centres are not received in time by the division. This further aggravates to the problem of students, as due to delay, grades of these assignments are not shown in the consolidated grade cards sent to students. As per information available to the researcher, university evaluates more than 20 Lac assignments in a year, which obviously is a difficult task to carry out timely with efficiency. Success of the assignment evaluation system of IGNOU to a great extent depends upon the effective coordination and communication systems in the university. University has to look for alternative means such as spot evaluation to overcome the problem of inefficiency in the system, which is very essential for retaining the confidence of students in the system.

Computer Marked Assignments

Computer mark assignments also form part of teaching-learning methodology in distance education system. The performance of students in computer mark assignments also counts in final grades scored by him.

Majority of respondents from Student Registration and Evaluation Division have stated that computer mark assignments are received directly at the headquarters. There exists no well-defined mechanism for receipt of assignments at Student Registration and Evaluation Division. Due to lack of proper mechanism in the Student Registration and Evaluation Division many assignments get misplaced, resulting in hardship to the students.

Therefore, it is once again suggested that university constitute a Database Management Systems and use the latest advancements in the field of computer and communication technologies to overcome the problem of efficiency and coordination. All the Learner Support Centres of university should be provided with computer and internet facilities so that they can directly transmit of assignments grades in time to the database management system, enabling the Student Assessment and Evaluation System to use that database for sending the consolidated grade card to the students in time. Similarly, students should also be provided the option of sending the computer mark assignments through e-mail. It will be helpful in overcoming the problem of feeding the assignments in computers and saving of processing time to a great extent. This facility will definitely facilitate the student's of computer and management programmes, who constitute a majority. Extensive use of computer technology and internet will prove efficient and cost-effective. It will reduce the manpower requirement, reduce the postal expenses and improve the performance by reducing the errors that take place in manual feeding of asignment grades.

Examination of project course at IGNOU

Students are allowed to take up project reports as prescribed in the programme curriculum after completing the minimum prescribed requirements. Student submits a project proposal and after its approval by university, prepares the project report within the deadlines prescribed by the university. After receipt of project, it is sent to the evaluator, who in turn is asked to send brief comment on the project separately for sending it to students for their information.

As the students submit project proposals in mass hence it is very difficult for the university to verify the originality of the proposal received from students. The project proposals received in the division are sent to the identified evaluators for evaluation. Feedback, which is recognized as an important aspect of teaching-learning methodology in distance education is not shared with the students. Therefore, to ensure compliance to the conceptual provisions of distance education, feedback from evaluator must be shared with the students. It seems that university is cutting short of procedure and failing in its duty to inform evaluator comments to the students.

Recently, SOCIS (School of Computer and Information

Sciences) has changed its evaluation strategy for the project proposals of the BCA and MCA programmes. Earlier the project proposals were submitted to the School for approval. Now as per the revised policy, they are submitted at the respective Learner Support Centre and after its approval at the Learner Support Centre, the final project after preparation is submitted at the SR&E Division. Again, it appears that all the pros and cons while designing guidelines are not carefully studied as there is every possibility to get the same project proposal approved at two different Learner Support Centres and copying of the project work of one student by the other or even more. Once, proposal has been duly approved by the learner support centres, university will not be in a legal position to take any action in the matter.

Inefficiency of the university in implementing its own decisions and frequent shift in policy without weighing the pros and cons of such changes results in further confusion among students and also wasteage of time and money as stabilization of changed process takes a long time.

Conduct of practical for term-end-examination

Practical examinations are conducted for science, computers, education and other professional programmes wherever prescribed. Student is required to have a minimum 75% attendance in practical sessions and in absence of required attendance students are not allowed to sit in the theory and practical examinations. University, considering the importance of practical examination appoints external examiners from the academic counsellors of that programme in consultation with Coordinators and Assistant Coordinators of the Learner Support Centres. They are responsible for providing examination facilities and counsellors for invigilation. They are also responsible for preparation of examination schedule, to decide the venue of examination, ensuring availability of adequate facilities like computers in case of computer programmes.

This shows how causally the university handles the conduct

of practical term-end-examination. These practical examinations are the most crucial component of examinations. University should take it seriously. Observers from the Regional Centres/headquarters must be deputed to supervise the conduct of practical examinations throughout the country. The present situation is based on mutual trust, which can be misused, and may bring bad name to the university. Presently, there is every possibility of a nexus between students and people from the Learner Support Centres. Otherwise, learner support centres of university are mostly located in private institutions and possibility of forming such a nexus is every possibility.

It is suggested that university should consider alternate strategies by studying the one used by Department of Electronics for its O, A, B, and C level programmes, or similar academic institutions for maintaining the sanctity of practical - examinations.

Term-End Examination System at IGNOU

Schools set up three sets of question papers for ensuing term-end examination and hand over the same to student assessment and evaluation division, which initiates the process of getting question papers printed confidentially. Simultaneously, tenders are also invited for procurement of answer-scripts. The process of identification of examination centres also goes on simultaneously depending upon the number of student's option to appear at a particular examination centre. Normally, all the Learner Support Centres are identified as examination centres and Coordinator of the centre is the examination superintendent, who is responsible for the safe custody of question papers and answer-scripts. The coordinator may nominate a senior faculty member as the examination superintendent well in advance.

The university supplies the sealed packets containing question papers to examination superintendents. These packets are to be opened in presence of invigilators and a certificate to this effect is recorded in the prescribed form. Each centre superintendent is supplied with a list of students showing their name and enrolment, who will be appearing at the centre.

Term-end examination carries 70 to 75% weight age in the final result as per provisions contained in the programme guide. The university conducts term-end examination twice a year i.e., June and December. Schedule of examinations is sent to all the learner support centres 5 months in advance. The same is also notified to through IGNOU Newsletter. All those students, who have paid their fees, opted and pursued the prescribed course, submitted the required number of assignments within due dates and have submitted their examination form to SR & E Division are eligible to appear in the term-end examinations. University sends hall-tickets to students indicating their examinations centres and dates of examination.

Majority of respondents from Student Registration and Evaluation Division have stated that hall-tickets for examination are sent 20 days before commencement of examination. The hall-tickets are sent to students by ordinary post. Hence, some of them do not receive their hall-tickets, which is essential for appearing in the examination. The students who submit their examination form with late fee are sent hall-tickets by registered post. Respondents have also stated that students are allowed to sit in the examination on production of identity card if their names are shown in the list sent by the university.

Conduct of term-end examination throughout the country is a massive exercise and requires excellent coordination for maintaining the sanctity of examinations. The respondents from Student Registration and Evaluation Division have indicated following mechanism for maintaining the sanctity of examination:

- The examinations are held as per the guidelines given in the manual on examination system of the university;
- The university has laid down rules and procedures and activities related to examination are closely monitored;
- The sanctity of examination is solely based on the

confidence, faith and sincerity of Centre Superintendent;

- Observers are sent from amongst faculty and Regional Centres.

It is correct that there are rules and procedures for conduct of term-end- examinations. Despite that, there have been instances of leakage of question papers and occurrence of such instances are on the increase. Majority of respondents from Student Registration and Evaluation Division have stated that there were instances of paper leakage in 1999, December 2000. Again there have been paper leakage in December 2001 and university had to cancel those papers and reschedule the same later. It is incorrect that university sends observers for conduct of term-end-examinations; however, observers are sent for entrance tests conducted by the university. The coordination mechanism for smooth conduct of examinations is coordination with Regional Centres, Centre Superintendent but this has started proving ineffective. Therefore, university should send all the teachers and academics for maintaining the sanctity and credibility of examination system. Otherwise, students will loose their confidence in the distance education system.

To overcome the problem of paper leakage in examination, university should take steps like sending observers from the teachers, academics and officers of the university to all the examination centres throughout the country. This may prove little costly, but it is essential for maintaining the credibility of the system among the student fraternity.

Evaluation of answer-scripts

University sends all the question papers for evaluation to the evaluators recommended by the School concerned. The respondents from Student Registration and Evaluation Division have affirmed that result declaration takes very long time. The results of previous term-end-examinations are not declared even after commencement of next semester examinations. Respondents from SR & E Division have opined that university should consider introducing the spot evaluation system to overcome the delay in evaluation of answer-scripts. This is despite the fact that university pays very handsome remuneration for evaluation of answer-scripts. It should, therefore, enforce for timely evaluation of answer-scripts. It is suggested that university should keep a panel of evaluators and those who delay the evaluation of answer-scripts should be blacklisted, for future and no answer-scripts be sent to them for evaluation.

Declaration of results

As, there is delay in evaluation of answer-scripts, the process of declaration of results is also delayed. The university intimates the results to the students and there have been reports of errors in declaration of results. Despite this university does not have a provision for revaluation.

Recently, courts have ordered for making the revaluation system mandatory for all the academic institutions. Hence university should introduce the policy of revaluation for its students.

Issue of consolidated grade card to the students

All the respondents from Student Registration and Evaluation Division have stated that it takes more than three months to issue consolidated grade card to the students. But it is a fact that many students do not receive their grade card even after 6 months as results are delayed. Sometimes, grade cards sent to students do not contain the grades of evaluated assignments. There are also errors in the grades of term-end examinations and assignments in the grade cards sent to the students. The centres should be required to send the assignment grades either to Regional Centres or to Database Management Systems through E-mail resulting in faster and accurate communication in cost-effective manner. This will also enable to overcome the problem of delayed receipts of assignment grades from learner support centres and help in timely issue of grade cards to the students.

Convocation

University holds its main convocation every year at headquarters and at all Regional Centres through teleconferencing simultaneously. Successful students are awarded degrees, diplomas and certificates, for which they have qualified. The system of holding parallel convocation through teleconferencing is good as it will be difficult for the students to come all the way for attending the convocation in Delhi. The chief guests are invited at all Regional Centres, who award the certificates to the successful candidates. The university should consider revising the process of convocation at the Regional Centres and visualize more active participation of the chief guests.

Suggestions for improving the performance of student assessment and evaluation system at IGNOU

Respondents have suggested for providing more infrastructure facilities keeping in mind the increased student enrolment and making training programmes as part of the systems for improving the performance of the officers and staff in the division. In addition, it is also suggested that policies and guidelines brought out by the Schools should be duly vetted by Student Registration and Evaluation Division for ensuring sanctity, fairness in evaluation work or all the guidelines related to assessment and evaluation are issued by Student Registration and Evaluation Division itself. The university should also consider deployment of teachers, academics and officers to examination centres as is being done in case of entrance tests to check the paper leakages and to maintain the sanctity of term-end examinations, practical examinations etc.

Chapter 9

CONCLUSIONS AND SUGGESTIONS

Education has been instrumental in disseminating various accomplishments of human civilization throughout human history in different forms. It has been recognized time and again that education plays a crucial role in producing and transferring knowledge and skills in society. Education contributes to economic growth, poverty reduction, development of mental faculties, and the growth of general awareness in all human societies.

Education systems in India have seen many changes i.e., from Gurukul, Madarsa and Convent/Public School education to the era of distance education and e-education. This transformation of education system is a continuous process world over. The system of distance education emerged to provide an effective alternative to the traditional system of education. It helps in diffusion of education and equalization of educational opportunities.

Distance education system has acquired the status of an important social organization after its fruitful existence of more than two decades since its evolution. It is making a valuable contribution in fulfilling the educational objectives of the society, with its advent as a viable supplement to the conventional education system.

In July 1962, first time in India, University of Delhi established Directorate of Correspondence Courses (later renamed as School of Correspondence and Continuing Education). In 1970, which was considered as International

Education Year, Ministry of Education and Social Welfare in collaboration with the Ministry of Information and Broadcasting, University Grants Commission and Indian National Commission for Cooperation with UNESCO, organized a seminar on the "Open University", which recommended for establishment of an Open University on an experimental basis.

The Govt. of Andhra Pradesh took initiative and established an Open University, the "Andhra Pradesh Open University" first time in the country in 1982 (now renamed as Dr. B.R.Ambedkar Open University). Encouraged by the success of establishment of an open university at state level, the Union Government also established "Indira Gandhi National Open University" by an Act of Parliament on September 20, 1985. The establishment of National Open University has been a welcome development because the impediments, which the traditional university system posed in the way of promoting distance education, could be surmounted.

Enthused by the success of distance education in the State of Andhra Pradesh and Indira Gandhi National Open University at national level, several State Governments also came forward with the idea of establishment of Open Universities in their States. As on date, nine State Governments have established open universities.

Quality of distance education programmes depends upon the distance education system and its management. The management of any educational system is nothing but the adaptations of a coordinated approach of all the functions/sub-systems used for delivering education to the learners enrolled for the purpose. The same principle also applies to distance education system.

Management of a dynamic distance education system has to grapple with a wide variety of issues and concerns. These include the mission and purpose of the system in the context in which it operates, the programmes and their curricula, the strategies for teaching and learning, the organization of the infrastructure for communication and interaction with students, the choice of technology, policies regarding students and staff, the development and distribution of study materials, funding and establishment of the credibility of the system itself.

The managers of distance education systems have to address their tasks to implement several integral components of a complex system. Distance education is an enterprise and exhibiting industrial features, the use of management techniques are much more appropriate. Distance education should be managed as system because of use of all human and technological resources are planned, it also has sub-systems within the systems, the most important of which are the design subsystems and those for instruction and learner support, evaluation and production. The management of such an institution requires interdependent sub-system, which involves constant administrative attention and teamwork. The management of distance teaching university involves four key elements i.e., planning, organizing, implementing and controlling.

The success of quality education initiative in distance education system is greatly dependent on the managerial factor. It is essential that top management of any learning system is completely committed to the concept and cause, and is able to visualize the future as a whole and take appropriate decisions. This means that mission of the educational institute has to be clearly defined, its long and short term objectives are clearly identified, strategies, coordination mechanism, financial provisions are accordingly planned.

Indira Gandhi National Open University, which was established in 1985 by an Act of Parliament to democratize higher education in the country, aims to provide cost-effective, quality education to the large population including those living in remote and rural areas. Following are the findings and suggestions with regard to the prevailing management of distance education system at Indira Gandhi National Open University.

Planning and Development Division of Indira Gandhi National Open University is responsible for framing policies and strategic plans for making the open learning system contextual and relevant. The university formulated its objective in 1985 without having any vision and mission, which is a prerequisite. The study suggests that the university should devise vision as well as mission to formulate policies. To have effective strategic planning and management of distance education system in the university the researcher has proposed the following mission:

"To accelerate the process of furtherance of comprehension, theoretical and practical both. To unwrap new vistas of knowledge and help the students in augmentation of vision, and engendering catholicity of views."

The policy formulation mechanism in the university should be on the basis of inputs received from different Schools and Divisions. Monitoring of implementation of plans should be continuous process and corrective measures as and when needed should also be taken for achieving the planned targets.

Planning and Development Division of IGNOU should play an important role in planning, policy designing and development of short-term plans, long–term plans, resource mobilization and in strengthening different sub-systems in the university and also by ensuring its adherence by all the sub-systems.

Long-term plans of the university are vague and fail to quantify the targets. The number of programmes to be launched during next five years, number of student enrolment during next five years, likely revenue generation and its utilization during next five years, utilization of surplus or how to meet the short fall in revenue collection should form part of five-year plans. Long-term plans should also address innovative and technology up gradation measures for next five years.

Administration Division in IGNOU looks after administration, which plays a crucial role in providing function and system support to the organization and all communication among sub-systems. Administration is responsible for management of human resources, financial resources and library system. Staff Training and Research Institute of Distance Education looks after the training and development function of IGNOU.

An appraisal of human resource management function in Indira Gandhi National Open University system reveals that university have not made any systematic and regular effort to design and implement effective policies in the area of human resource management. There is lack of proper coordination and systematic effort for training and development of different categories of staff at IGNOU. Therefore, it is suggested that university must have separate human resource division and all the planning with regard to human resource management in this division must be a regular feature. Organization of human resource management activities needs planning and implementation system. Strategy and policies in the area of human resource should be part of system and most important to have the control system for monitoring the human resource activities.

Education in India to an extent depends upon government funding, donations etc. Public funding on education in recent times, especially in the field of higher education has been declining and it has become essential to explore alternate channels of funding. This has also influenced the financial management of government institutions like Indira Gandhi National Open University.

The basic objective of financial management should be cost-effectiveness, increased output, and higher rate of return on investment with efficiency in student services. The Finance Committee of the university is responsible to look after on the whole financial management function of the university. It consists of the Vice-Chancellor as its Chairman, Finance Officer and other members nominated by the Vice-Chancellor including a representative of the Ministry of Human Resource Development.

Finance and Accounts Division of IGNOU is responsible for collection of revenue receipts on behalf of university, payment to staff and outside suppliers, preparation and approval of budget estimates from the Finance Committee and Board of Management. To have effective financial management system, it is essential to monitor the collection of revenue receipts from time to time to ensure that it is accounted properly and expenditure is also related with the income. Hence, it is must to monitor the revenue periodically as it helps in ensuring proper accounting of the same.

The study on the basis of appraisal of the functioning of Finance and Accounts Division strongly suggests for improving the performance of F & A Division. Computerization will help in strengthening the financial management and personnel matters in the university. Wide area network (WAN) connectivity with Regional Centres centres will help in on-line accounting and faster reconciliation and finalization of annual accounts of the university.

Distance education is more attuned to learning than teaching, therefore, library has central place in the distance education system. Library at IGNOU operates through three-tier system; central, regional and local. Students of IGNOU must be informed about the facilities and services available to them at regional and learner support centre libraries, so that they can avail of these facilities according to their need. Library staff of IGNOU should also be given proper training for organization and management of libraries.

In order to improve the access of library to the student community there is also a need for proper planning and coordination between central, regional and learner centre libraries. For proper utilization of libraries, they should be opened on weekends. The process of decentralization of procurement of book and generals and delegation of financial and administrative powers to Regional Centres needs to be expedited. For improving the performance of library division, it should be provided adequate staff, space and infrastructure facilities to become digital/electronic library.

Major concerns of university's programmes are its academic offerings. Academic programmes are developed to fulfill the thirst of knowledge of a population segment. The basic objective of acquiring knowledge is to settle in life by acquiring professional and other kind of certification to get a job for his or her lifetime. Planning and Development Division of the University works in cooperation with the Schools in providing them with relevant information and assisting them in developing their proposal as specific projects for consideration at various levels. At present 64 programmes are being offered by 9 Schools of the University.

Most successful programmes launched by the university attracting large student enrolment are from the School of Computer and Information Sciences and School of Management Studies having 50% and 15% enrolment respectively. Remaining 55 programmes comprises 35% of student enrolment indicating that all these programmes lack in market demand and usefulness in development of human skills. The researches on programme evaluation, system evaluation should form part of School's duties and responsibilities for improving the quality of academic programmes.

Distance education system before the advent of electronic media was considered a passive mode of instruction lacking in interest and enthusiasm leading to boredom. Modern science and technology has placed variety of electronic based instructional aids at the disposal of the educators and learners that play a significant role for a developing country like that of ours in reaching the un-reached. Communication media and technology have changed the total scenario in distance education system by improving the quality of instruction. Newer technologies like audio-video, CDs, television, radio and teleconferencing etc., have provided an added advantage to the distance education in reaching the un-reached population segment. The technology has helped in cutting the distances between institutes and the learner. Another, important advantage of technology is that it helps in maintaining the standards of quality in distance education material in media components, which is a powerful medium of delivery. Technology component may be costlier initially but finally distance education is cheaper than conventional education system.

The planning of media activities in IGNOU should start from root to higher level. More administrative staff be sanctioned to handle the increased workload due to launch of Gyan Darshan and Gyan Vani. Professionals in advisory/policy planning should be included for proper planning of media activities.

Research plays an important role in effective management of distance education system. The efficiency of all managerial functions is dependent on inputs in the form of information, which assists decision-making, organizing and effective implementation of the decision. The research policy of the university is to promote subject based and discipline based areas, developmental studies, interdisciplinary studies and system based areas. Distance education system is a new field of education and has enough potential for research on various aspects of systems development and programme evaluation.

The research can play a crucial role in strengthening and development of distance education system. Researches undertaken at Indira Gandhi National Open University should be aimed at system improvement, programme evaluation and identification of judicious mix of different kind of media used in the system. This will help in bringing real cost-effectiveness for which distance education system is known.

In a distance education system students have to be provided with a wide range of services. These services include access to information about programmes, courses, how and when to enroll, whom to contact for tutorial guidance and advice, where to pay fees and where to sit for examinations and so on. Unlike the traditional system, in which the student generally have uniform levels of attainment, motivation and commitment, the open learning system usually has a vastly heterogeneous body of students. They are from diverse backgrounds, with varying levels of prior educational attainments, and their objectives are vastly different to fit any single pattern of attitudes, and behaviour. The managers of the open learning system have therefore to take all these factors into account while designing and organizing the student services sub-systems.

Student Registration and Evaluation Division look after student registration function in Indira Gandhi National Open University. The information regarding commencement of admission reaches all over the country through newspapers advertisements in national and local dailies, through telecast on educational channel and broadcast on radio. In addition to this, Regional Centres also make local arrangement for wider publicity regarding commencement of admissions of the university like using Cable TV and distribution of handout through learner support centres. This helps the university in reaching the un-reached areas and makes them aware about the educational programmes offered by IGNOU for advancement of learning.

Admission form cum prospectus for all the programmes offered by the university are available at Regional and Learner Support Centres. However, filled in forms along with fees and testimonials are received at the Regional Centres, which are responsible for carrying out admissions. The forms for the programmes having entrance examinations like management, information technology are received at SR&E Division; admission forms for B.Ed. are however received at the Regional Centres itself. The university should devise a uniform policy for receipt of admission forms for all the programmes either at Regional Centres or at Student Registration and Evaluation Division.

Student's handbook-cum-prospectus provides complete details of its admission process, course curriculum, and evaluation methodology and examination system. Every effort should be made to use simple language so that applicants find it easy to understand.

Besides effective management of student registration in any distance education institution, the timely, accurate and correct flow of information is also important for the decision making process which in turn is essential for effective management. The university has a large amount of student data, examination data, assignment-evaluation data, evaluator's data and other kinds of data of other systems, which need to be maintained. Maintenance of a large data should be on the principles of database management system.

Database management system can help in timely organization of activities and effective control of activities though management information system. Database Management System in Indira Gandhi National Open University can maintain the data on programmes, courses, students, finances, counsellors, coordinators, staff, materials, inventory control, library acquisitions etc. Every sub-system in the university should have easy and quick access to relevant information, for which an effective Management Information System as sub-system of Database Management System must be managed effectively.

In distance education system, study material plays a vital role in supplementing face-to-face interface between the learner and teacher. Study material helps learner in easy understanding of the subject matter and self-test exercises help in self-evaluation to the learner.

University should consider decentralization of distribution of study material to Regional Centres, which will help in overcoming the problem of delay in despatch of study material resulting in reduced number of student's complaints. It may also prove cost-effective if on the spot admission is ensured and students submitting their applications in person are supplied study material in person. This will also improve access to students, as Regional Centres are closer to the students in comparison to the Material Printing and Distribution Division. It will also help in reducing the number of errors, which occur in transmission of data to Student Registration and Evaluation Division.

The management of student support services is an uphill task in distance education system. Indira Gandhi National Open

University uses the network consisting of Regional Centre and Learner Support Centres. Learner Support Centres include different kind of delivery channels depending upon the need of the programme and strategy to reach the un-reached. Student support services sub-system is probably the most difficult sub-system to manage. These include coordinators, programme in-charge, counsellors, tutors and line managers and periphery staff of Learner Support Centres and the staff at Regional Centres. The counsellors, who constitute the long-standing staff at Learner Support Centres, provide counselling, tutorial and evaluation support to the student. The tutor, who is subject expert, provides resource materials, gives feedback on assignments, advises on personal and career problems, and generally encourages students. The coordinator of Learner Support Centre is responsible for looking after the tutorial services at the grass-root level. Staff at the Regional Centre, headed by the Regional Director, plays the crucial role of monitoring the functioning of the Learner Support Centres. It provides feedback to the headquarters and relays back advice and instruction to the centres. Management of these personnel, who must work in coordination, requires skill, tact and patience.

Many States have established their own Open Universities and student enrolment in these States puts a question mark on the viability of establishing Regional Centres in these States as it results into double expenditure on the same activity. Therefore, it is suggested that university should devise a policy for establishment of Regional Centres considering the changed scenario of upcoming State Open Universities.

Regional Services Division is also responsible for monitoring the activities of the Regional and Learner Support Centres. The university has expanded a lot during last decade in terms of Regional Centres, Learner Support Centres and student enrolment. To keep the system strengthened and efficient, it is essential that extensive monitoring of activities of Regional and Learner Support Centres is carried out. Monitoring system needs to be clearly defined and should be mandatory for all Regional and Learner Support Centres. Proper feedback should also be provided on the monitoring reports so that centres can improve upon their performance. Lack of monitoring in the division has also affected the delivery of student support services, audio-video services, teleconferencing services, and library facilities.

In order to provide effective and timely student support services by IGNOU to the students, organizational restructuring should be undertaken at the earliest for effective and efficient coordination and communication systems. The structure of university should be in pyramidical form and headquarters should only concentrate on policy, planning, reviewing, resource allocation, audit, programme evaluation and student evaluation and research. All activities aimed at students should be decentralized with commensurate delegation of powers. Database Management Systems should be restructured for strengthening coordination and communication across the sub-systems in the university.

In any distance education system, the institution providing academic programmes-services is also involved in assessment of learners and management of processes of learner evaluation. This learner evaluation consists of student assessment (assignment evaluation) and term-end-examination. Assessment evaluation involves the marking and grading of assignments, providing advice in the form of comments, and speedy return of the graded material to the student. Casual correction, without meaningful comments and delay in return of assignments may lead to loss of interest and increase in number of dropouts. Hence, it is necessary to ensure that assignments are properly evaluated and for this encouragement and motivation from tutors are necessary.

Procedure followed by open universities for the conduct of term end examination, and the evaluation of answer-scripts, is similar to that of conventional universities. Management responsibilities are those related to secrecy in setting up of question papers, its proper moderation, fair conduct of examinations at the centres, prompt despatch of answer-scripts to headquarters, appointment of competent examiners and prompt examination of answer-scripts. Subsequent steps are tabulation of marks and declaration of results.

Student assessment (assignment evaluation) at IGNOU is done through Learner Support Centres, whereas Student Registration and Evaluation Division looks after the function of term-end-examination. Performance of students in IGNOU is evaluated on the basis of assignments submitted by them, on the basis of term-end- examination conducted at the end of minimum duration prescribed for the course/programme, on the basis of execution of specific projects, field works, seminars, practicals or any other technique for assessment to determine the level of performance of students pursuing different courses/ programmes.

For making more effective management of student assessment and evaluation system at IGNOU, it is suggested that more infrastructure facilities need to be provided in order to evaluate ever-increasing student enrolment and more training programmes should be organized for improving the performance of officers and staff in Student Registration and Evaluation Division. Last but not least, there should be more effective proper coordination between Student Registration and Evaluation Division, Regional Centres, Learner Support Centres and Examination Centres of the university.

Future of Distance Education

In the recent years, open and distance education has acquired considerable significance all over the world. In this context, the quality of operation of system and its sub-systems has come to the centre stage of discussion. In order to ensure the quality of distance education it is necessary to look into the managerial aspects of the system as well as its sub-systems.

The system of distance education helps in diffusion of education and equalization of educational opportunities. The population in India is increasing rapidly and formal means of education have failed to keep pace with it. In a developing country like India, where large number of people are deprived of educational opportunities due to poverty, distance education can serve as a mean for providing and equalizing educational opportunities by utilizing its multi-media approach.

Distance education system has wide scope for emerging learning society in general and educationally underdeveloped or developing societies. It is capable of acting as a useful medium for promoting diversified as well as vocational professional education. Distance education is a source of inspiration for those who had "dropped out" at some stage or the other. The scope of distance education is very large and it is capable of serving vast and varied clientele.

Presently, we are passing through the age of information technology. The impact of new technology has helped in improving distance education system. With advanced communication technology, teaching-learning process has become faster and interesting as compared to that in conventional education. Distance education is the front-runner in exploiting the potential of information technology so as to reach the learners to teach them while assuring also its future, especially in the third world countries like India.

The future of distance education lies in absorption of latest technology as well as careful planning, organizing, implementation of different sub-systems and putting appropriate control mechanisms in place to check deviations.

To make the teaching-learning process effective in distance education system, what are needed are efficient planning, organization, implementation and control in all its spheres. From the analysis, it is seen that what is needed is the application of management processes and functions in the system and sub-systems created and managed for achieving the desired objectives. The sub-systems also require proper restructuring, delegation and decentralization of responsibilities. Roles and responsibilities are needed to be clearly defined for improving productivity and efficiency in the system. Database Management System and Management Information System needs to be introduced and implemented for improving coordination and communication in the sub-systems of the university. This will result in improved functional efficiency and goal attainment.

Distance education system has come as a boon for the developing countries of the world like ours. The problem in our country is of numbers due to incomparable explosion in population. Distance education system is the answer to provide education to all that too in qualitative form as it has the capacity and potential to enforce the principles of management for delivering quality education to the students.

BIBLIOGRAPHY

1. Sharma, Yogendra, K (2001) *History and Problems of Education,* Vol. 1, Kanishka Publishers, Distributors, New Delhi, p. 373.

2. Altbatch, P.G. (1987), *Higher Education in Third World, Themes and Variations,* Sangam Books, London, p. 3.

3. George Thomas Kurian, (1987) *Encyclopedia of Third World.* 3rd edition. Vol.4, New York. Facts on file inc. p. 1052.

4. Dohmen, G (1977) *Das Fernstudium, Ein Neues Pedagogisches Forschungs-und Arbeitsfeld.* Tubingen: DIFF.

5. Holemberg, B. (1981) *Status and Trends in Distance Education,* Kogan Page, London.

6. Wendemeyer, Charles. A (1977)) *Independent Study.* A.S. Knowles (ed.)

7. Peters, Otto (1973) Dies Didaktische "Structure des Fernunterrichts. Unterschungen zu einer Industrialisierten Form des Lehrens and Lerners. Weinnheim:Beltz.

8. Moore, M.G (1973): 'Toward a Theory of Independent Learning and Teaching'. *Journal of Higher Education* 44, pp. 661-679.

9. Project Report, IGNOU (1985), Ed.CIL. New Delhi.

10. Planning Commission (1960) *Third Five-Year Plan 1961-66,* Govt. of India , New Delhi.

11. (1961) *Proceedings of the 28th meeting of the CABE,* Publication No. 591, Govt. of India, New Delhi

12. (1962) Report of the Expert Committee on Correspondence Courses, Ministry of Education, Govt. of India, New Delhi.

13. Report of the Working Group on National Open University, (1971) Govt. of India, New Delhi. (Unpublished)

14. (1982) Establishment of Open University in the State, Constitution of a Committee to Work out the Details of the Project, G.O.Ms. No, 4494, May 25, Govt. of Andhra Pradesh, Hyderabad.

15. Gazette Notification, (1982) The Andhra Pradesh Open University Act, 1982, G.O. No.870 Edn.October, 30, Govt. of Andhra Pradesh, Hyderabad.

16. IGNOU Act (1985), Govt. of India, New Delhi:

17. Open Universities in India (2000) Brief Information, Distance Education Council, p. 21, Indira Gandhi National Open Univ., New Delhi.

18. Murgatyard and Andrew Woud (1989) "Issues in Management of Distance Education," *American Journal of Distance Education*. Vol. 3. (1).

19. Holemberg, B. (1982) *Recent Research into Distance Education*, 2, Volume, Fern Universitat, (ZIFF).

20. Shashi (1972) A Comparative Study of Achievement of Students Passing through Correspondence Courses and Regular Courses, M.A. dissertation, Kurukshetra University, Kurukshetra.

21. Robinson, B.S. (1989) *Indira Gandhi National Open University: Integrating Higher Education Reform with National Development Goals*, Doctoral Dissertation, University of Massachusetts, Massachusetts.

22. Kaul, Lokesh (1986) *Methodology of Educational Research*, Vikas Publishing House Pvt. Ltd, New Delhi

23. Kothari, C.R. (2000) *Research Methodology, Methods and Techniques*, Wishwa Prakashan, New Delhi. p.39

24. IGNOU Act, (1985) IGNOU, New Delhi.

25. Profile (2000), Indira Gandhi National Open University, New Delhi, p. 8.

26. Profile (2000), op. cit., p. 9

27. Profile (2000), op. cit., p. 10

28. IGNOU, Planning and Management of Distance Education, (2000), New Delhi, p. 53.

29. Planning and Management of Distance Education, op. cit., p. 54.

30. Planning and Management of Distance Education, op. cit., p. 54

31. Cole, GA. (1993) *Management Theory and Practice*, 4th edn, DP Publication, London.

32. IGNOU, Educational Systems Management, (2000), New Delhi, p. 9.

33. Educational Systems Management, op. cit., p. 9.

34. Educational Systems Management, op. cit., p. 10.

35. Jenkins, G.M. (1969)'A System Study of Petrochemical Plant", *Jour. System Engineering* 1, p. 99.

36. Dearden, John, (1972) "MIS is a Mirage", *Havard Business Review*, p. 99.

37. Makridakis Spyros, (1971)" The Whys and Wherefores of the Systems Approach" *European Business*, Summer.

38. Forester, Jay (1961) *Industrial Dynamics*, The MIT Press, Cambridge, pp. 5-6.

39. *Educational Systems Management*, op. cit., pp. 8-9.

40. IGNOU, Planning and Management of Distance Education, New Delhi.

41. IGNOU, Planning and Management of Distance Education, New Delhi, p. 61.

42. IGNOU, Planning and Management of Distance Education, New Delhi, p. 62.

43. Profile (2000), IGNOU, New Delhi, p. 51.

44. Crawford, F. (1991) Total Quality Management, *Occasional Paper,* CVCP, London, 8pp.

45. Shukla, Madhukar, (1996) *Understanding Organizations: Organizational Theory and Practice in India,* p. 24.

46. Longnecker, J.G. (1973), *Principles of Management and Orgnisational Behaviour,* Columbus, Ohio, Charles E. Merril Publishing Co.

47. Fayol, Henry (1949), " Industrial Engineering and General Administration", J.A.Coubrough, Geneva, Switzerland, International Management Institute, 1929, p. 17.

48. Otto Peters (1973) Dies didaktische "Structure des Fernunterrichts. Unterschungen zu einer Industrialisierten Form des Lehrens and Lerners". Weinnheim: Beltz.

49. Profile (2000), IGNOU, New Delhi, p. 42.

50. Profile (2000), op. cit., p. 57.

51. IGNOU, Educational Systems Management, New Delhi, p. 63.

52. Educational Systems Management, op. cit., p. 63.

53. IGNOU, Planning and Management of Distance Education, New Delhi, p. 75.

54. Profile (2000), op. cit., p. 46.

55. Profile (2000), op. cit., p. 46.

56. Profile (2000), IGNOU, New Delhi.

57. IGNOU, Planning and Management of Distance Education, New Delhi, p. 76.

58. Planning and Management of Distance Education, op. cit., pp. 76-77.

59. Profile (2000), IGNOU, New Delhi

60. IGNOU, Planning and Management of Distance Education, New Delhi, p. 60

61. Planning and Management of Distance Education, op. cit., p. 61.

62. Powar, K.B., Panda Santosh and Bhalla Vina (2000), Performance Indicators in Distance Higher Education, Aravali Books International Pvt. Ltd, New Delhi, p. 57.

63. Powar, K.B., Panda Santosh and Bhalla Vina (2000), op. cit., p. 58.

64. Profile (2000), IGNOU, New Delhi, p. 48

65. Profile (2000), op. cit., p. 49.

66. Powar, K.B., Panda Santosh and Bhalla Vina (2000), op. cit., p. 59.

67. Profile (2000), op. cit., p. 52.

68. Diversified Delivery System, 2000, Scheme of Partner Institutions, Regional Services Division, IGNOU, New Delhi, p. 5-6.

69. Powar, K.B., Panda Santosh and Bhalla Vina (2000), op. cit., p. 60.

70. Powar, K.B., Panda Santosh and Bhalla Vina (2000), op. cit., p. 61.

71. Profile (2000), op. cit., p. 53.

EXHIBIT I

Programmes on Offer at IGNOU

Research Programme

1. Ph.D. in Education
2. Ph.D. in Social Sciences

Masters Degree Programme

3. Masters of Arts in Distance Education
4. Masters of Business Administration
5. Masters of Business Administration (Banking and Finance)
6. Masters in Computer Applications
7. Masters in Library and Information Science
8. Masters in Tourism Management
9. Masters of Arts in English
10. Masters of Arts in Hindi

Bachelors Degree Programme

11. Bachelor of Arts
12. Bachelor of Commerce
13. Bachelor of Science
14. Bachelor in Computer Applications
15. Bachelor of Education
16. Bachelor in Information Technology
17. Bachelor in Library and Information Sciences
18. Bachelor of Science in Nursing
19. Bachelor of Technology in Civil (Construction Management)

20. Bachelor of Technology in Civil (Water Resources Management)
21. Bachelor of Tourism Studies

Post Graduate Diploma Programmes

22. Post Graduate Diploma in Financial Management
23. Post Graduate Diploma in Human Resource Management
24. Post Graduate Diploma in Management
25. Post Graduate Diploma in Marketing Management
26. Post Graduate Diploma in Operations Management
27. Post Graduate Diploma in Distance Education
28. Post Graduate Diploma in Higher Education
29. Post Graduate Diploma in Maternal and Child Health
30. Post Graduate Diploma in Hospital and Health Management
31. Post Graduate Diploma in Rural Development
32. Post Graduate Diploma in Translation
33. Post Graduate Diploma in Journalism and Mass Communication
34. Post Graduate Diploma in International Business Operation

Advance Diploma Programmes

35. Advance Diploma in Information Technology
36. Advance Diploma in Tourism Studies

Diploma Programmes

37. Diploma in Creative Writing in English
38. Diploma in Creative Writing in Hindi
39. Diploma in Early Childhood Care and Education
40. Diploma in Management

41. Diploma in Nutrition and Health Education
42. Diploma in Tourism Studies
43. Diploma in Primary Education (Module I)

Certificate Programmes

44. Diploma in Youth in Development Work
45. Post Graduate Certificate in Radio Writing
46. Certificate in Disaster Management
47. Certificate in Environmental Studies
48. Certificate in Food and Nutrition
49. Certificate in Human Rights
50. Certificate in Computing
51. Certificate in Guidance
52. Certificate in Labour Development
53. Certificate in Nutrition and Child Care
54. Certificate in Participatory Forest Management
55. Certificate in Consumer Protection
56. Certificate in Rural Development
57. Certificate in Teaching of English
58. Certificate in Teaching of Primary School Mathematics
59. Certificate in Tourism Studies
60. Certificate in Empowering Women Self-Help Groups
61. Certificate in Women's Empowerment and Development
62. Certificate in Participatory Project Planning
63. Certificate in Youth in Development
64. Certificate in Rural Surgery

Preparatory Programmes

65. Bachelor's Preparatory Programme

EXHIBIT 2-A

A SYSTEMS MODEL OF DISTANCE EDUCATION SHOWING THE MATERIALS AND STUDENT SUB-SYSTEMS

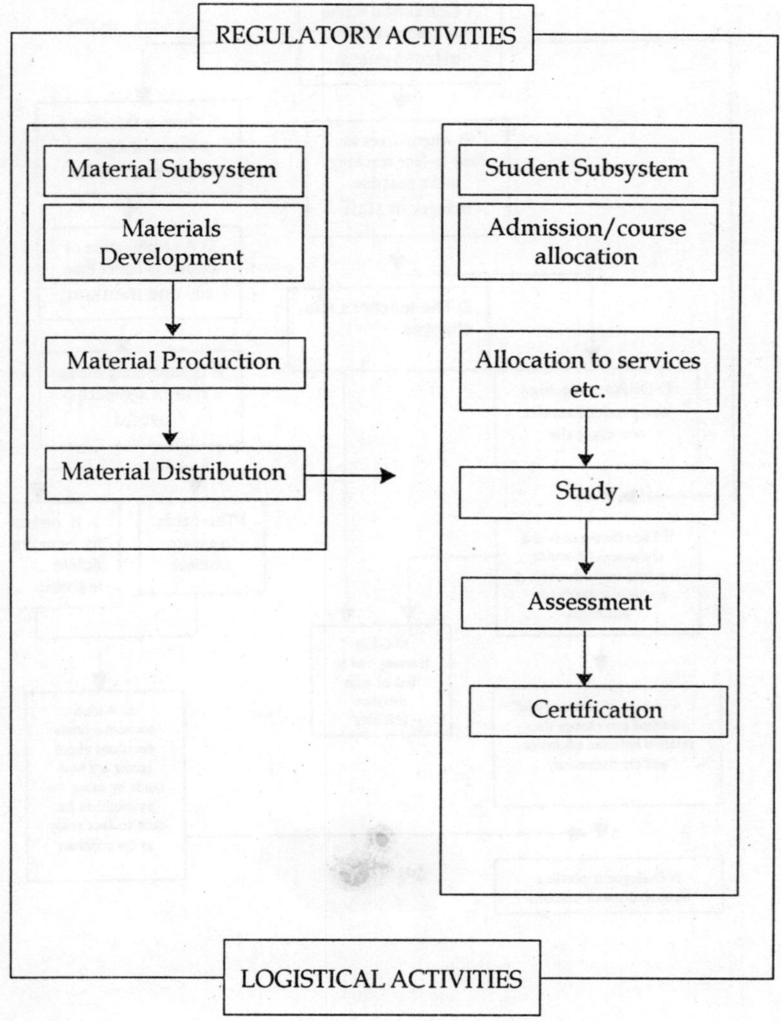

Source: The Planning and Management of Distance Education, Greville Rumble (1986).

EXHIBIT 2-B

A HOLISTIC MODEL OF DISTANCE EDUCATION

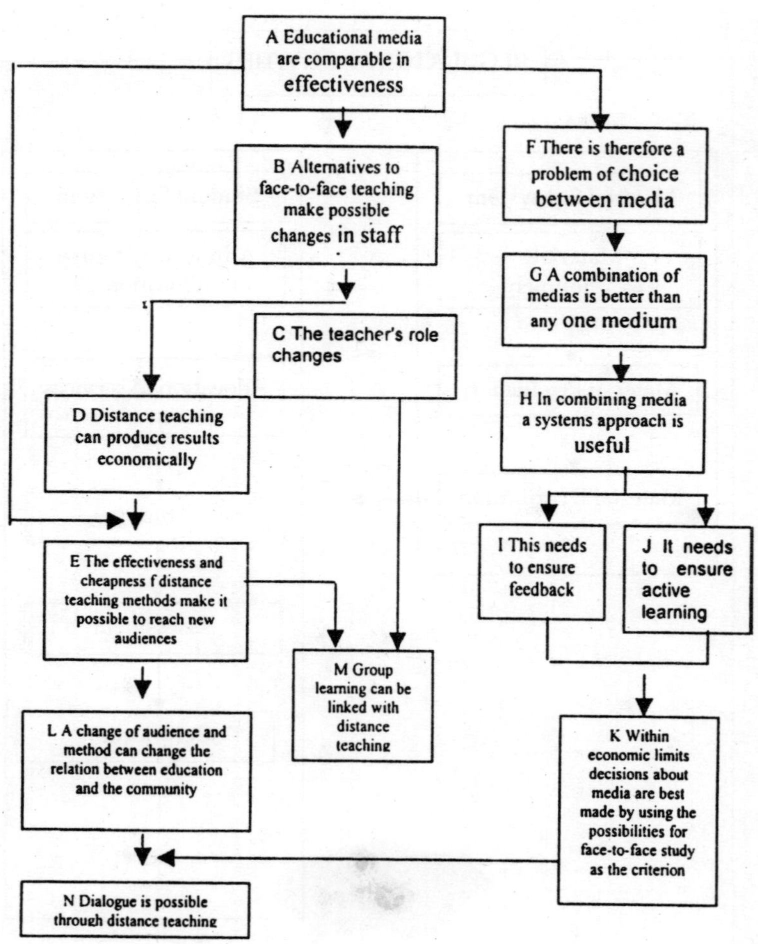

From H. Perraton (1981) 'A theory for distance education', Prospects, 11 (1), p. 23.

EXHIBIT 2-C

A TRANSACTIONAL MODEL OF DISTANCE EDUCATION

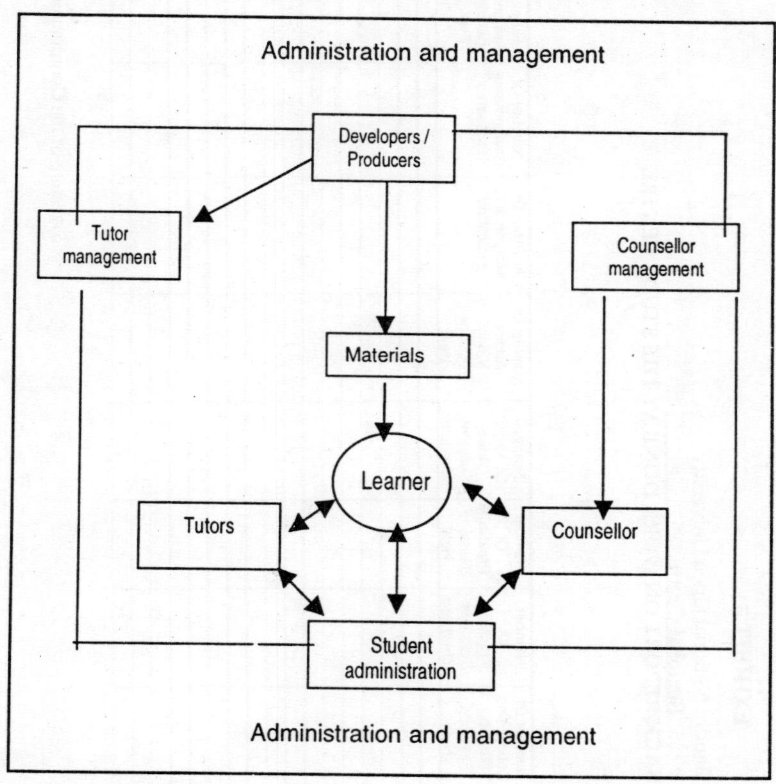

Source: Henir, F. and Kaye, A. (1985) 'Enseignement a distance-apprentisage autonome? in Henri, F. and Kaye, A. (eds.) (1985) Le savoir a domicile: predagogie et pronblematique de la formation a distance, Quebec, Presses de l'Universite du Quebec/Tele-universite.

EXHIBIT 3

Indira Gandhi National Open University

Regional Centre, ____________

MONTHLY FEEDBACK REPORT ON WORK DONE AT THE STUDY CENTRE

STUDY CENTRE: ____________________

REPORT FOR THE MONTH OF: ____________________________

S No	Programme Semester	Number Of Students Enrolled	Course	Number Of Counselling (Theory) Sessions Scheduled	Number Of Counselling (Theory) Sessions Held	Number Of Practical Sessions Scheduled	Number Of Practical Sessions Held	Number Of Audio/ Video Sessions Scheduled	Number Of Audio/ Video Sessions Held	Number Of Assignments Submitted	Number Of Assignments Evaluated	Number of Assignments pending for Evaluation
	TOTAL											

(If necessary additional sheet may be attached)

Date:

Signature of the Coordinator

INDEX

H

I

L

M

O

P

Q

R